35 Best Books for Teaching U.S. Regions

by Toni Buzzeo and Jane Kurtz

S C H O L A S T I C
PROFESSIONAL BOOKS

New York • Toronto • London • Auckland • Sydney
Mexico City • New Delhi • Hong Kong • Buenos Aires

Dedication

With thanks to Franny Billingsley, and Richard, Miranda, and Nathaniel
Pettingill, for opening their home to us, feeding us, and inviting us to sing
while we wrote this book.

Acknowledgments

We would like to thank author Gloria Rothstein for her book, *Read Across
America*, which spurred us to realize our idea could become a reality.
Thanks, too, to our editor, Virginia Dooley, for her warm and smart support.

Note

Educators who wish to contact Toni Buzzeo about conference and
staff development speaking engagements may visit her Web site at
www.tonibuzzeo.com.

Cover design by SOLÍS Design & Production

Cover and interior art by Dave Clegg

Interior design by Sydney Wright

ISBN: 0-439-20763-0
Copyright © 2002 by Toni Buzzeo and Jane Kurtz
All rights reserved. Printed in the U.S.A.

Contents

Introduction

About This Book

We can remember exactly when *35 Best Books for Teaching U.S. Regions* sprouted in our minds. We were part of a fiction writers' retreat at Popham Beach, Maine, when we were joined at breakfast by a principal from a New England school. After she was introduced to the writers from Maine, North Dakota, Iowa, Maryland, Massachusetts, and Illinois, she said, "Do you know what schools really need? They need a resource for novels set in different geographic regions all across the United States." We looked at each other and nodded.

For each of the seven U.S. regions featured in this book, we recommend fifteen books and include background, resources, and activities for five of those books, all of which are available in paperback. In all the bibliographic information, we provide the paperback publisher (when available) and the original copyright date. We also note when a book is available in an audio recording.

It was important to us that the books reflect the interesting mosaic of the North American experience, so we included many cultures, time periods, and perspectives. Occasionally a book's settings span several regions. (Take, for example, *The Watsons Go to Birmingham—1963*, in which the characters travel from Flint, Michigan to Birmingham, Alabama, and back again.) Such books muddy the waters a bit, but they can also be a rich resource for comparisons. While we encourage you to use them wherever they fit best for you, we placed them in the region where most of the activities were centered.

How to Use This Book

We've designed the book for maximum flexibility. If you group states into regions different from ours, use the state designations at the beginning of each chapter to set up your own regions. Explore all the books in the seven regions if you have time, work with one or two books from each region, or concentrate on a single region—whatever fits your needs.

We recommend that you consider three possibilities for using the five focus novels: reading them aloud to the whole class, buying a classroom set so every student can read the novel individually, or dividing the five novels among literature discussion groups. We encourage you to support students' reading opportunities across each U.S. region by stocking your classroom library with the additional titles, book pairings, and suggested resource books. In addition, you will want to alert your school library media specialist (and perhaps your public librarian) to the titles in the regional bibliographies as well as in the book pairings.

Notes on On-Line Resources

We have tried to include only large, long-standing Internet sites and to offer several sites whenever possible, knowing the ephemeral nature of the World Wide Web. We will keep an updated list at **http://www.janekurtz.com** and **http://www.tonibuzzeo.com**. Note also that occasionally in background suggestions we include a book that is no longer in print; you will need to ask a school or public librarian to interloan these books or try to locate them through on-line booksellers, such as Amazon.com. Finally, when you cannot find book-based information appropriate to the region you're studying, look to the Internet as a way to communicate with schools in other regions. The "HotList of K–12 Internet School Sites—USA" at **http://connectedteacher.classroom.com/library/states.asp** will help you make connections.

* Please preview sites listed for student reference to make sure the material is appropriate for the developmental level of your students.

Missing May
Cynthia Rylant
Yearling, 1992

Listening Library

Summary
Twelve-year-old orphan Summer has lived with her Aunt May and her Uncle Ob for six happy years when May suddenly dies in her garden. Ob and Summer are bereft at her loss. For six months, with the help of Summer's eccentric classmate, Cletus Underwood, they struggle to pull the fabric of their lives together despite the hole May's absence creates. Finally, they leave their mountainside home in Deep Water, West Virginia, to find a way to contact May and the strength to go on living without her.

Background
Cynthia Rylant was born in Hopewell, Virginia, and by the age of four had moved to live with her grandparents in a house without electricity or running water in the remote West Virginia town of Cool Ridge. They rarely went anywhere because her grandparents had no car. She lived there until she was eight, when her mother finished nursing school. Then she and her mother moved to the southwestern West Virginia town of Beaver. Although Rylant went on to college, earning a degree in library science at Kent State University in Ohio, many of her books, like *Missing May*, are based on her...

Book Pairing
When May was nine years old, her family was killed in a flash flood in Ohio. Compare this flood and the way it affected the main character to the flood that takes place in *The Day it Rained Forever* by Virginia T. Gross (Middle Atlantic section, page 33).

Find Out More
About the author To learn more about Rylant, visit the Education Paperback Association Web site biography at http://www.edupaperback.org/authorbios/Rylant_Cynthia.html.

Literature guides You can find these guides to *Missing May* on the Web:
★ A teaching guide written by Marilyn Joyce on the Information Literacy Projects site at the University of Maine, Department of Computer Science at http://www.umcs.maine.edu/~orono/collaborative/missing.html.
★ A set of discussion guides for Missing May at the Ohio Literacy Resource Center at http://literacy.kent.edu/Oasis/Pubs/0300-16.html.

Whirligigs For background information on whirligigs, visit the Science Museum of Minnesota Web page, "From Windmills to Whirligigs" at http://www.sci.mus.mn.us/sln/vollis/index/frontvollis.html

Hands-on Activities

Design a whirligig: Two Representations (page 41) Ob designs and builds whirligigs. Some, called "The Mysteries," represent abstract ideas like Love, Dreams, and Death—they are not yard decorations, but art. Talk to students about the difference between concrete art, which represents a figure or scene you can identify, and abstract art, which does not represent things but, like Ob's art, represents ideas and feelings.

Let students explore the difference between these two ways of representing as they work to design two whirligigs that reflect their reading of *Missing May*. Have them use the space to the left on page 41 to design a whirligig that represents a character, object, or scene from the book, such as a landmark from West Virginia. Then have them use the space to the right to design an abstract whirligig that shows an idea or feeling from *Missing May*. (Encourage them to use line, color, texture, and shape to show the idea, rather than to draw a realistic picture.) Extend the exercise by providing students with recycled materials to make their whirligigs three-dimensional or have them design a new cover for *Missing May* in which they incorporate both whirligig designs.

Map it Using a model map of West Virginia and the clues from the story, have students create a route map of the trip that Ob, Summer, and Cletus take from Deep Water to Charleston. Remind students that Glen Meadows is not an actual town. They'll need to put it in a logical spot on their maps. Direct them to Chapters 9 and 10 for clues that will help them decide where Cynthia Rylant intended for Glen Meadows to be.

WV trip plans Invite students to design a travel brochure similar to the Triple A guide Ob, Summer, and Cletus consult before

capital, Charleston, West Virginia. What sights will students recommend that the characters be sure to see in this state? Have students use the places mentioned in Ob, Summer, and Cletus's travels in *Missing May* and from their own research on West Virginia to design a trifold travel brochure that could be mailed to the characters. For information on Charleston, refer students to the West Virginia Legislature home page at http://www.s.state.wv.us/. Click on the Kids Page link on the left and read the Activities Book online or download it.

A picture tells a thousand words Cletus collects pictures that tell a story ("Anything with a story to it," he says on page 18) and keeps them in a suitcase. Create a storytelling picture collection file with interesting photographs and/or magazine and newspaper picture clippings. Let each student choose one of the pictures from the collection and write a story to go with it, as Cletus always encourages May to do for his pictures. Encourage them to bring their characters to life the way Cletus does the "Brylcreem guy" in Chapter 13. Students can make a connection to *Missing May* by setting their stories in West Virginia or by using other details from the book. Keep this collection of picture prompts available for students to access during independent writing.

Terrific titles Cletus loves the newspaper title that accompanies the photo of Reverend Miriam B. Young: "The Reverend Miriam B. Young: Small Medium at Large." He tells Ob and Summer, "I'd dearly love to write newspaper titles when I'm grown" (page 52). Give students a chance to play with words and capture the main idea of three favorite pictures from the class picture collection (see activity above). Have them write their clever titles for the pictures on index cards and post all of the pictures around the pictures on a bulletin board for classmates to contrast and enjoy.

Feel free to photocopy or read aloud sections of these pages for students. You may want to photocopy the pages for a particular book to distribute to students or keep in a class reference folder a copy of all the pages for books in a specific region.

Watch for the icon to identify titles available as audiobooks through Recorded Books or Listening Library.

Teacher resource pages To help you create a rich reading experience for students, we've provided summary, background, and resource information about each featured book—including online and in-print author information and background information on the time period, culture, or setting. The Hands-on Activities section offers creative ways to help students process the information they've learned and use additional resources to explore themes and topics introduced in the book. The activities emphasize the following skills and concepts:

★ Geographic concepts and skills

★ Learning from literature through reading and writing

★ Critical thinking skills in different content areas

★ Internet research skills

Student activity pages Most sets of resource pages are followed by a student activity page that invites students to think critically about the featured book and make important connections to literature. Copy and use this activity page with students during or after they read the featured book.

Design a Whirligig: Two Representations
Missing May

Ob designs and builds whirligigs. His whirligigs, "The Mysteries," are abstract, meaning they show ideas or feelings like Love, Dreams, and Death, rather than people or objects. In the spaces below, design two whirligigs: In the box on the left, draw a whirligig that shows a character, animal, place, or landmark that reminds you most about *Missing May*—your concrete representation. In the box on the right, draw a whirligig that shows an idea or feeling from *Missing May*—your abstract representation.

whirligig—concrete representation: character, animal, place, or landmark	whirligig—abstract representation: an idea or feeling

New England

★ **Vermont to Massachusetts**
Lyddie by Katherine Paterson
(Puffin, 1991)

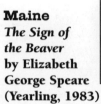

★ **Maine**
The Sign of the Beaver by Elizabeth George Speare (Yearling, 1983)

★ **Maine**
Fire in the Wind by Betty Levin (Beech Tree, 1997)

★ **Connecticut**
Junebug by Alice Mead
(Yearling, 1995)

★ **Massachusetts**
Becoming Felix by Nancy Hope Wilson (Avon Camelot, 1996)

Other Recommended Regional Readings

★ **Connecticut**
Windcatcher by Avi (Avon Camelot, 1991)

★ **Maine**
Calico Bush by Rachel Field (Aladdin, 1966)

★ **Massachusetts**
Seth and Samona by Joanne Hyppolite (Yearling, 1995)

The Witch of Blackbird Pond by Elizabeth George Speare (Yearling, 1958)

★ **Rhode Island**
The Art of Keeping Cool by Janet Taylor Lisle (Atheneum, 2000)

★ **New Hampshire**
A Gathering of Days by Joan W. Blos (Aladdin, 1979)

Heart of a Chief by Joseph Bruchac (Dial, 1998)

★ **Northeastern Woodlands**
Guests by Michael Dorris (Hyperion, 1994)

★ **Vermont**
A Day No Pigs Would Die by Robert Newton Peck (Random House, 1972)

Faraway Summer by Johanna Hurwitz (Avon, 1998)

 Recorded Books

Junebug

Alice Mead

Yearling, 1995

 Book Pairing

Alice Mead sets the sequel to this novel, *Junebug and the Reverend* (Farrar, Straus & Giroux, 1998), after the family moves to the new apartment building. It is Junebug's job to take the grouchy reverend in apartment 6-A on a daily walk. Junebug learns more about himself and his relationships with others in the process.

Summary

At nine years old, Reeve McClain (Junebug) is approaching his tenth birthday with apprehension. He's been somewhat protected until now by childhood, but at ten, in the New Haven, Connecticut housing projects, a boy becomes something else—a helpmate to drug dealers and gang members, or a target of them. Despite the difficulties in his life, Junebug, who cares for his little sister Tasha after school while his mother works long hours, is an optimistic boy who dreams of learning to sail and, finally, of escape from the projects.

Background

Many people in America live in housing projects, which fall under the umbrella formally known as subsidized housing. According to the Department of Housing and Urban Development, there were more than five million subsidized housing units in our country in 1998. A third of the people who live in subsidized housing are elderly and more than half are minorities. Two-fifths are, like Junebug's, single parent families with children. Eighty-five percent of people in our country have one or more subsidized housing units right in their own neighborhood.

Find Out More

About the author Students may want to know what life experiences led Alice Mead to set Junebug's story in a housing project in an East Coast city. Encourage them to contact the author from her homepage, "Alice Mead, Author of Real Interesting Books for Kids" at **http://home. maine.rr.com/alicemead/**. (Since authors often find it difficult to answer numerous individual letters, have students compose letters in groups or write a single class letter, instead.)

History of housing projects Junebug lives in a housing project, yet some students may not know much about housing projects, or how public housing came into being. If you'd like more information yourself, read the article, "Franklin's Monster Destroyed; An overview and analysis of the demise of public housing" at **http://cses.com/rental/franklin.htm**. Statistics about public housing are also available from the Housing and Urban Development site in the article "A Picture of Subsidized Households in

1998" at **http://www.huduser.org/datasets/ assthsg/statedata98/index.html**.

Hands-on Activities

City or state map? City maps and state maps pose different challenges for students. Invite them to explore the size, geography, boundaries, and scale of the city and state in which Junebug lives. You can request a map from the city of New Haven at the Greater New Haven Convention and Visitors Bureau, 59 Elm St., New Haven, CT 06510. State maps are available from the Connecticut State Department of Tourism at 1-800-282-6863. Now help students compare the features on the two maps. What do the maps have in common? What features does the city map have that are not included on the state map, and vice versa?

Plan a trip *Junebug* gives us a glimpse of one part of New Haven, Connecticut. Challenge students to plan a five-day trip to New Haven. In addition to visiting with Junebug, what else would they like to do while they are in the Elm City? Write to the Greater New Haven Convention and Visitors Bureau, 59 Elm St., New Haven, CT 06510 for tourism information or use the following Web sites to provide students with ideas: The City of New Haven Online at **http://www.cityofnewhaven.com/today/index. html** and Greater New Haven Convention & Visitors Bureau at **http://www.newhavencvb.org/**.

Script a new ending *Junebug* ends hopefully as Junebug's family plans to leave Auburn Street Project for a new place near Mama's new job at the group apartments for the elderly program. Challenge students to think of other ways that the novel could have ended. As a class or individually, have students develop an alternate last chapter for the novel.

Help the homeless An important issue raised in this book is that not all children in the U.S. enjoy a safe, comfortable, or stable home. (Treat this issue with sensitivity, as some of your students may live in unsafe or unstable environments.) Design a classroom project to help the homeless in your community. You may ask people in your town or city hall for advice. Or if you choose to use the Internet, investigate the Department of Housing and Urban Development's Web Site for Kids. Their page on helping the homeless will give your students some project ideas at **http://www. hud.gov/ kids/hthsplsh.html**. Encourage students to post the story of their project on the Web site.

Memory book for Junebug Throughout this book, Alice Mead describes the buildings, grounds, and neighborhood of the low-income housing project where Junebug lives. Read aloud or have students find and share several such descriptive passages. Using these descriptions, help students create a scrapbook of scenes from the book, focusing on the Auburn Street Project. What is Junebug's environment like?

50 wishes bulletin board Junebug's dream is to release 50 bottles onto the ocean on his tenth birthday. Each bottle will contain a wish. On a bulletin board with butcher or craft paper, create an ocean of waves. Now, design one or more bottles from cellophane and staple them to the board, creating a pocket with each bottle shape. Have students write several wishes on small pieces of paper, fold them, and enclose each wish in the pocket of each bottle shape on the bulletin board, so that your display shows 50 bottles filled with students' wishes.

Invite a speaker Contact the community agency that helps with housing in your town or city. Ask someone to come to speak to your class about housing, or homelessness, in your community. Have students prepare questions based on what they've learned from reading *Junebug* and from their own experiences with homeless people.

Becoming Felix
Nancy Hope Wilson
Avon Camelot, 1996

Summary

Twelve-year-old JJ Jaquith loves both his family dairy farm in western Massachusetts and his clarinet. He struggles to define his allegiance to each as his parents work to keep the farm solvent, and his music teacher and best friend encourage him to develop his musical talent. Almost daily, he swings between the need to give up jazz to devote himself to the farm and the need to sacrifice his dream of farming in order to pursue his music. The stakes grow higher and his friendships—as well as both of his passions—are threatened.

Background

Nancy Hope Wilson worked once a week for a year on a dairy farm in order to ground her writing of *Becoming Felix* in reality. She asked the farmer she worked for to treat her as he would a twelve-year-old boy, which he did. It was a great experience for Wilson; in fact, throughout this time, she felt as though she had dairy farming in her blood.

The novel is set in the fictional village of West Farley, which Wilson says is based on West Hawley, Massachusetts. The nearby university town of Hampton is based on Amherst, Massachusetts.

Book Pairing

Are other family farms like JJ's? Broaden students' understanding of life on a farm with this nonfiction picture book about a Wisconsin family dairy farm owned by five generations of Petersons: *Century Farm: One Hundred Years on a Family Farm* by Cris Peterson (Boyds Mills Press, 1999).

Find Out More

Life on a dairy farm Find a list of Massachusetts dairy farms open for visits at the "Dairy Resources" page at New England Dairy Council **http://www.umass.edu/umext/mac/resource_lists/dairy.htm**. If there is a farm or a ranch in your area of your region, arrange to take a field trip to visit for the day. If possible, arrange for the class to spend some time with the farmers or ranchers themselves. Prepare students by discussing the difficulties and rewards the Jaquith family faced in *Becoming Felix* and have them prepare interview questions to take along on the trip.

Moooo-re milk, please! Visit the MooMilk site at **http://www.moomilk.com/**. Students will enjoy learning more about dairy farming as they go on the The Story of Milk virtual tour, take the Moo Milk Quiz, play the Connect the Dots game, and enter the What's the Cow Thinking contest. Read the FAQs (Frequently Asked Questions) at this great dairy industry site!

Hands-on Activities

Graphic organizer: To Farm or Not to Farm (page 11) Use this graphic organizer to help students compare the benefits and the disadvantages they've read about farming in *Becoming Felix*. Encourage students to add to what they've learned in the book with their own research (you'll find resources mentioned in the Background and Find out More sections above). Another student-friendly site related to farming is the Farm School site **http://www2.kenyon.edu/projects/farmschool/addins/homepage.htm**.

Map it The Jaquith family lives in the Connecticut River Valley area of western Massachusetts. Have groups of students create a physical map of the area. If you would like to use the Internet as a resource, try the UMassK12 site at **http://k12s.phast.umass.edu/~masag/watershed/topomap.html**. Follow up the mapmaking with a discussion about what makes this area of New England a good place for dairy farming.

Farm work bulletin board In *Becoming Felix*, students will encounter the names of much of the equipment necessary to run a modern dairy farm. Create a bulletin board with a large-scale picture of JJ's family farm, illustrated by students. Make sure to have them include the house, the barns, the fields and hills, and even turtle rock. After doing research in your library media center, have students illustrate each of the following pieces of farm equipment and place it on the farm illustration where it would be used. Students can find photographs of the machinery at the John Deere site at **http://www.deere.com/** (use the Equipment Quick Find feature). Have them label each piece of equipment, and in a sentence, tell what it is used for.

mower (30)	hay baler (31)
corn chopper (31)	manure spreader (31)
plow (31)	cultivator (31)
tedder (31)	harvester (48)
silo unloader (88)	

A letter to Benny Goodman What would JJ like to ask Benny about the struggle he's in, or about his music? What might Benny Goodman have written in response? Ask students to think about these questions and write an exchange of letters from JJ to Benny Goodman. They can find out more about JJ's musical hero at the Benny Goodman, King of Swing site at **http://www.davidmulliss.com.au/BennyGoodman/benny.htm**.

Comparison chart JJ's dog Sketch is a Border collie. Books and articles about the Border collie breed will help students understand why Sketch is the perfect dog to live and work on a dairy farm. If you choose to use the Internet, check out the All About Border Collies site at **http://www.bordercollie.org/core.html**. Have students list all of the traits of the Border collie and then research another of the herding breeds, such as the German shepherd, the Australian shepherd, or the Old English sheepdog, at the Digital Dog site at **http://www.digitaldog.com/herdingdogs.html**. Then have them list the traits of that breed compared to the traits of the Border collie. Help students organize their information by using a T chart. Students may fill in the chart with other important characteristics.

Express your opinion After students have read *Becoming Felix* and understand some of the issues facing family farms, they may feel compelled to write for more information to the Committee to Save the Family Farm, 466 Chestnut Street, Ashland, MA 01721-2299. When they have formed an opinion about the issue, encourage them to write an editorial for their local paper or to a state legislator, including what they have learned and the opinions they formed while reading *Becoming Felix*.

To Farm or Not to Farm?

Becoming Felix

There are both benefits and challenges to living on a family farm, as you have see in *Becoming Felix*. Use both the ideas that you have gathered from JJ's story, as well as ideas you may gather from your own research, in order to fill in the T chart below. If you would like to use the Internet for your research, you will find great information at the <u>Farm School</u> site at **http://www2.kenyon.edu/projects/farmschool/addins/homepage.htm**.

Benefits of Life on the Family Farm	Challenges of Life on the Family Farm
+	**–**
+	**–**
+	**–**
+	**–**
+	**–**
+	**–**

The Sign of the Beaver

Elizabeth George Speare

Yearling, 1983

 Listening Library

Summary

After building a cabin in the Maine territory and planting a crop of corn and pumpkins, 12-year-old Matt Hallowell's father leaves him alone while he returns to Quincy, Massachusetts, to fetch his wife and other children and bring them to the new homestead. As Matt counts the long weeks his father is gone, he suffers many difficulties. Luckily, a young Penobscot boy and his grandfather befriend Matthew while he struggles to learn the skills he needs to survive in the wilderness.

Background

Elizabeth George Speare was a native New Englander, a fact that influenced many of her books, including *Sign of the Beaver*. Born in 1908, she was raised in Massachusetts, which seemed to her the perfect place to grow up, and spent her entire life in New England. After marrying, she moved to Connecticut, where she raised her two children. In addition to *Sign of the Beaver*, which is set in colonial Maine territory, two other of her books, *The Witch of Blackbird Pond* and *Calico Captive*, are also set in colonial New England. Speare reported that she actually felt at home in colonial times, since rural New England had not really changed much in three hundred years! It is no wonder Speare's novels have such a strong sense of place.

 Book Pairing

The Sign of the Beaver works on several levels—as a book about Penobscot Indian life, as a book about Colonial settlement of New England, and as a survival story. Pair this novel with another survival story, *Toughboy and Sister* (Pacific section, page 107) by Kirkpatrick Hill.

Find Out More

About the author Find out more about Elizabeth George Speare in the article "Speare, Elizabeth George" at the Educational Paperback Association site at **http://www.edupaperback. org/authorbios/Speare_ElizabethGeorge.html**.

The Penobscot Nation Learn about the history of the Penobscot Nation at the Indian Island School site at **http://challenge.ukans.edu/ Indian-Island/commun.htm**.

Milo, Maine How has Milo changed since the arrival of European settlers in Maine? Find information about this modern-day town, at the Milo Historical Society site at **http://www. kynd.com/~milohist/history.htm**.

Hands-on Activities

Graphic Organizer: Matt's Wilderness Survival Skills (page 14) Use this graphic organizer to help students identify the survival skills Matt brought with him to Maine from Massachusetts and those which he learned from Attean and the Penobscot people. Extend the classification by having students fill in the Other Solutions column with ways they imagine Matt could have managed without the knowledge he had.

Map it Invite students to create a map of the trip that Matt and his father take from Quincy, Massachusetts, to their new land in the Maine territory. Pay close attention to the description of their route in Chapter 1. Have models of route maps, such as the hand-drawn route map in *Journey to Nowhere* (Middle Atlantic section, page 24), available for students to consult as they design their own.

Classify Maine's animals Because Matt is living very close to nature, he encounters more than twenty different animals in this book, all animals of the north woods. First, have students read through the book and make a list of these animals. Then, using a chart like the one below, they can classify the animals according to their group (mammal, bird, insect, fish). Extend the activity by letting students sort these animals by other categories, such as size and potential use as food.

Mammal	Bird	Insect	Fish

Animals-by-state bulletin board On a bulletin board, mount two state maps, one of Maine and one of your home state. Have students draw a picture of each of the animals they have read about in *Sign of the Beaver*. Invite them to list on an index card five facts about the animal they've illustrated. On or around the Maine map, have students place their drawings of the animal. Place fact cards under each picture. Repeat this process for animals that live in your home state and mount them on your state map with five facts about each.

Design a field guide Matt finds at least eight different kinds of trees (pine, hemlock, maple, birch, aspen, ash, spruce, oak) near his new home in the Maine territory and puts them to many different uses. Support students as they research each of these trees and learn more about its size, its nuts or seeds, and its uses. Encourage them to create a field guide for new Maine territory settlers. The field guide might include a drawing of the full tree, its leaves, and its nuts; information on size, shape, and color; and facts about its uses, which students will have learned both from research and from reading about the uses Matt makes of them in the novel.

Create a model cabin Matt and his father build a log cabin for their family to live in. Speare describes the cabin in great detail. Have students refer to her description, and any other information they find about building a log cabin, either to draw a picture of the interior and exterior of the cabin or construct a three-dimensional model cabin. Students can visit the "Building a Log Cabin: An Illustrated Guide" page at the Geocity site at **http://www. geocities.com/ RainForest/Canopy/2415/cabin1.html**.

From the Penobscot's point of view By the end of this story, Matt has come to understand the complicated issues involved in the settlers' habit of purchasing land. Challenge students to write a persuasive essay from the Penobscot perspective that argues against the settlers' right to purchase the land on which the Penobscot live and hunt. Remind students to open with a statement of their opinions and then offer at least three reasons why this should not happen. Encourage them to use facts from their research and from the book.

Matt's Wilderness Survival Skills

The Sign of the Beaver

Matt was able to survive because of the skills and knowledge he brought with him to Maine from Massachusetts and because of the skills and knowledge he learned from Attean and the Penobscot people. In the chart below, make a list of these skills and identify each as something Matt already knew or something Attean taught him. Then try to imagine what else Matt could have done, without the knowledge he had or the knowledge he gained from Attean.

Skills	Brought to Maine from Massachusetts	Learned from Attean	Other Solutions
Staying dry in the rain		How to make a birchbark poncho	Construct a rain shelter from woven saplings covered with pine needle boughs.

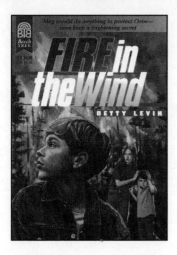

Fire in the Wind

Betty Levin

Beech Tree, 1997

Summary

Meg's role in the family is to defend her cousin Orin, who is "slow," and her younger brother Paul, who is tormented by the schoolyard bully. But when the Fire of 1947 breaks out in her home state of Maine, she has other things to worry about: whether she can get along with Uncle Frank and Aunt Helen in her extended family home now that Mom and Dad are gone much of the time, whether there really is an escaped POW or spy living in Mrs. Trilling's summer home, and whether her promise to Cousin Champ to look out for Orin includes keeping Orin's enormous secret.

Background

Betty Levin has a special connection with Maine. While she was born in New York City and grew up there as well as in Bridgewater, Connecticut, and Washington, DC, she summered for more than twenty years in Castine, Maine, and now summers in Brooksville, Maine, not far from the location of the 1947 wildfires on Mt. Desert Island.

Book Pairing

What's it like to live through a wildfire—and fight it? Help build students' background knowledge with these books on wildfires and fire fighting: *Fire in Their Eyes: Wildfires and the People Who Fight Them* by Karen Magnuson Beil (Harcourt, 1999) and *Fire: Friend or Foe* by Dorothy Hinshaw Patent (Clarion, 1998).

Find Out More

About the author For more information on Betty Levin and her books, see the WPL Maine Writers Index at **http://www.waterboro.lib.me.us/ maineaut/km.htm.**

The Fire of '47 To learn more about the Fire of 1947, read *Wildfire Loose: The Week Maine Burned* by Joyce Butler (Down East Books, 1997).

Invite a speaker Invite the local fire chief or a firefighter to your classroom to discuss the methods for fighting wildfires and how these may differ from fighting fires in buildings in cities or towns.

Hands-on Activities

Map it Encourage students to locate on a state map the following Maine communities, which were heavily damaged by the fires: Brownfield, East Brownfield, Hiram, Newfield, Goose Rocks Beach and Cape Porpoise (Kennebunkport), Fortune's Rocks (Biddeford),

Alfred, Kennebunk, Lyman, Waterboro, East Waterboro, South Waterboro, Dayton, and Bar Harbor (on Mt. Desert Island).

Chart 38 historic fires Students can create a map of the United States on a poster or large sheet of craft paper. A resource such as the Web article "Historic Wildland Fires and Their Impact" at **http://www.cnr.colostate. edu/FS/westfire/historic.html** will help them map the 38 historic fires in the United States. Have students add notes to the map that show the number of acres or homes destroyed and the number of lives lost.

Fires-around-the-country atlas As students read *Fire in the Wind*, have them create an atlas of wildfires organized by region of the country. They can mark the fires with their dates on a map of each region and, below, list as many details about each fire as possible (including such facts as dates of burning and loss of property and/or life). Go to the "Wildfire Central" page of the <u>Firehouse.com</u> Web site at **http://www.firehouse.com/wildfires/**. Check for the most recent accounts of wildfires across the country.

Read all about it! Tell students to imagine that they are reporters writing the newspaper story about Orin's heroism in saving his cousins and his family's barn. Remind them to open with a strong lead paragraph that answers the five W's: who, what, when, why, and where.

My dictionary of fire-fighting terms Invite students to create a dictionary of fire and fire-fighting terms using an encyclopedia article such as "Fire Department" in *World Book Encyclopedia*, the glossary in the back of *Fire in Their Eyes*, the "Glossary of Wildland Fire Terms" Web page of the National Interagency Fire Center at **http://www.nifc.gov/fireinfo/glossary.html**, or the "Internet Engine and Hose Fire Terms" Web page of <u>Emergency-World</u> at **http://www. emergency-world.com/eh/terms.htm**. They should select terms that apply to the story told in *Fire in the Wind* and identify the chapter where the term appears (or could have appeared) in the story. An entry might look like this:

> **Fire break** a natural or constructed barrier used to stop or check fires.
> *Orin was helping to dig trenches that would act as fire breaks in Chapter 7.*

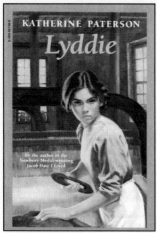

 Recorded Books

Lyddie
Katherine Paterson

Puffin, 1995

 Book Pairing

In the 1800s and early 1900s in this country, many children worked to support their families and themselves. They labored daily in unsafe conditions for long hours, a situation modern American children can't imagine. To give students an understanding of Lyddie's work environment, read *Bobbin Girl* by Emily Arnold McCully (Dial, 1996). Students may also gain a broader understanding of children's working conditions by reading *Kids On Strike!* by Susan Campbell Bartoletti (Houghton Mifflin, 1999).

Summary

When Lyddie's father abandons the family to seek fortune away from the Vermont farm, he leaves Lyddie with the care of her unstable mother, her younger brother Charlie, and her two tiny sisters. Together Charlie and Lyddie eke out a living as long as they can until their mother leaves and rents out the farmland. Lyddie then makes her way to Lowell, Massachusetts, where she works as a mill girl, encountering the many hazards and inequities of mill life and struggling to find her place in a new world.

Background

Katherine Paterson was born in and spent her first four and a half years in China. She has lived in more than thirty homes in three countries during her life and has set her stories in many different places. As a New England resident (she now lives in Vermont), Paterson uses her knowledge of her regional surroundings to focus some of her historical fiction work in this region.

Find Out More

About the author You'll find much information about Katherine Paterson at The Official Katherine Paterson Website at **http://www. terabithia.com/**.

Lowell mills The following sites invite students to research the history of the Lowell mills. They can explore different topics, including daily life, jobs, working conditions, and the town of Lowell.

★ Lowell National Historical Park at **http://www.nps.gov/lowe/loweweb/ Lowel_History/prologue.htm**

★ Modern History Sourcebook: "Harriet Robinson: Lowell Mill Girls" (primary source) at **http://www.fordham.edu/halsall/mod/ robinson-lowell.html**

★ The Illinois Labor History Society at **http://www.kentlaw.edu/ilhs/lowell.html**. (See "Factory Rules from the Handbook to Lowell, 1848"; "Massachusetts Investigation into Labor Conditions"; "A Description of Factory Life by an Associationist in 1846"; and "Boarding House Rules from the Handbook to Lowell, 1848.")

Hands-on Activities

Graphic organizer: Lowell, Massachusetts—Then and Now (page 19) Help students learn about the post-Industrial Revolution change that's occurred since the time when mill girls like Katherine Paterson's Lyddie worked in Lowell. Students may use this comparison chart to compare Lowell of 1843 with present-day Lowell in the areas of occupations, housing, and education. Feel free to add additional categories. Encourage students to use details from their reading of *Lyddie* and their research to fill in the Lowell of 1843 column. Students can research modern-day Lowell through several links from the Commonwealth Communities Lowell site at **http://www.state.ma.us/cc/lowell.html**, read about the city at the Lowell City Hall homepage at **http://web.ci.lowell.ma.us/**, or call the Massachusetts Office of Travel & Tourism at 1-800-227-MASS and request information.

Map it Lyddie travels from somewhere near Putney, Vermont, to Lowell, Massachusetts. After obtaining maps from the Massachusetts Office of Travel & Tourism at 1-800-277-MASS and the Vermont Department of Tourism and Marketing at 1-800-VERMONT, have students map out her route by foot and by coach.

Make a poster Show students photographs and maps of nineteenth-century Lowell, and then have them create a poster or wall display. Draw boarding houses and mills and use cross-section drawings to show their interiors and the equipment in the mills. You'll find great information in the nonfiction book *Mill* by David Macaulay (Houghton Mifflin, 1963).

"A day in the life" journal Read aloud or have students find and read "Massachusetts Investigation into Labor Conditions," an on-line article about a mill girl's daily schedule at the Illinois Labor History Society Web site at **http://www.kentlaw.edu/ilhs/lowell.html**. They can use that information to create a journal of one mill girl's week in Lowell. Suggest that they describe her schedule each day for one week, marking the dates at the top of the entries. Ask them to try to imagine what it was like to work the hours she worked and to have the boarding house meals and limited free time she had.

Sing a song of protest Because working conditions were so bad for girls in the Lowell mills, many girls joined the labor movement and sang protest songs. Read aloud the one that appears in the novel.

Oh! Isn't it a pity such a pretty girl as I
Should be sent to the factory to pine away and die?
Oh! I cannot be a slave,
I will not be a slave,
For I'm so fond of liberty
That I cannot be a slave. (p. 92)

Use this song as a model. Have students apply the information they have learned about mill life in their research and their reading of *Lyddie* to compose their own protest songs.

Lowell, Massachusetts—
Then and Now

Lyddie

Lowell, Massachusetts, has changed dramatically since the time when mill girls like Katherine Paterson's Lyddie worked there. Use this comparison chart to compare Lowell of 1843 with present-day Lowell.

Category	Lowell 1843	Lowell Today
Occupations		
Housing		
Education		

Middle Atlantic

Featured Regional Readings

★ **New York**
Falcon's Egg
by Luli Gray
(Yearling, 1995)

★ **New York**
Journey to Nowhere
by Mary Jane Auch
(Yearling, 1983)

★ **Pennsylvania**
The Cabin Faced West
by Jean Fritz
(Puffin, 1991)

★ **Rhode Island to Maryland**
Homecoming
by Cynthia Voight
(Ballantine, 1996)

★ **Pennsylvania**
The Day It Rained Forever by
Virginia T. Gross
(Puffin, 1991)

Other Recommended Regional Readings

★ **Maryland**
Anna All Year Round by Mary Downing Hahn
(Clarion, 1999)

★ **New York**
The Arrow Over the Door by Joseph Bruchac
(Dial, 1998)

The Cricket in Times Square by George Selden
(Yearling, 1960)

*From the Mixed-Up Files of Mrs. Basil E.
Frankweiler* by E. L. Konigsburg (Yearling,
1967)

My Side of the Mountain by Jean Craighead
George (Puffin, 1988)

Scorpions by Walter Dean Myers
(HarperTrophy, 1988)

★ **New Jersey**
Captain Grey by Avi (HarperCollins, 1977)

★ **Pennsylvania**
The Bread Sister of Sinking Creek by Robin
Moore (HarperTrophy, 1990)

Wringer by Jerry Spinelli (HarperTrophy, 1997)

*Dear Austin: Letters from the Underground
Railroad* by Elvira Woodruff (Random House,
1998)

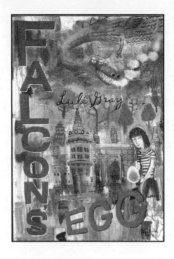

Falcon's Egg
Luli Gray
Yearling, 1995

Summary

When Falcon—Emily Falcon Davies—is eleven years old, she finds a large, red, glowing hot egg on the Great Lawn of Central Park in New York City, where she lives. Even though she knows she probably shouldn't, she can't resist "kidnapping" the egg. She takes it to the apartment of her best adult friend, Ardene, and with the help of the Friends of Egg, including her Great Aunt Emily and Freddy, an ornithologist from the Museum of Natural History, she protects and studies the egg. Emily struggles with her own feelings of being different and her family problems while she learns about the need for freedom and being true to one's own nature.

Background

Before moving to Chapel Hill, North Carolina, Luli Gray was a longtime resident of Manhattan. It's not surprising, then, that *Falcon's Egg* is rich with details of this borough of New York City. Surrounded by water, the 28 square mile island of Manhattan teems with a population of one and a half million people. It is the cultural heart and commercial center of the Big Apple. When we see the familiar New York City skyline in movies, we are looking at the Manhattan skyline!

For a folk-art view of New York city, introduce *My New York* by Kathy Jakobsen (Little, Brown, 1993).

Find Out More

About the author Not much information is available about Luli Gray. However, *Publishers Weekly* ran an interesting piece about her when *Falcon's Egg* was published, "Flying Starts: Three Children's Novelists Talk About Their Fall '95 Debuts." *Publishers Weekly*, December 18, 1995, pp. 28–30. You may be able to borrow it by library interloan.

Manhattan Take some time to get to know the big-city setting of *Falcon's Egg* by having maps and tour guides of Manhattan available for students to browse. You can view eight different Manhattan maps on-line at the New York Department of Transportation site at **http://www.ci.nyc.ny.us/html/dot/html/ transportation_maps/home.html** and select from twenty-four different maps at the Best of Manhattan site at **http://www.bestof.net/ manhattan/maps/**. Order the Official NYC Guide and the Official NYC Travel Planner from the NYC Convention and Visitors Bureau at 1-800-NYC-VISIT. You can also help familiarize students with Emily's surroundings in the Big Apple by visiting the PBS site, which features "New York, a Documentary Film Online" at **http://www.pbs.org/wnet/newyork/**.

Hands-on Activities

Map it The following places are listed in the novel. With a map of New York City as their guide, students can create a wall map of Falcon's neighborhood and identify these places. Invite students to illustrate the scenes that take place at the marked locations and attach the drawings to the map.

Great Lawn in Central Park
Belvedere Castle
Rumpelmayer's (St. Moritz Hotel, 50 Central Park South, between Fifth and Sixth avenues)
16 West 77th Street (Falcon's building)
Museum of Natural History (Central Park West at 79th Street)
East 66th Street (Aunt Emily's building)
Conservatory Garden, 105th Street
Korean deli on 77th Street and Columbus Avenue
Billy's on 89th Street
Pet store on West 74th Street
Central Park West
Central Park Zoo (64th Street and Fifth Avenue)

Big Apple trip plans Let students design a travel brochure for people visiting New York City. Feature several of the locations and attractions found in the mapping activity above. The opening text in the brochure should be a paragraph that convinces the tourist that New York City is the best vacation destination.

Vocabulary exploration On the Fourth of July weekend, Falcon and Aunt Emily do the *The New York Times* crossword puzzle. There are many unusual words in *Falcon's Egg*, perfect for crossword puzzle making. Divide the class into four groups and split up the word list below so that each group uses thirteen of the words to create a crossword puzzle. (Make sure enough dictionaries are available for each student or pair to use and that students have copies of the book to use for reference.) For each word, the clue should be the definition from a dictionary that matches the usage in the novel. Have students

include the page number the word occurs on along with each clue, so that the other groups who do their puzzle can look it up and use context clues for help. If you like, you can create your crossword puzzle at the Discovery School's Puzzlemaker site at **http://puzzlemaker.school. discovery.com/**.

essences (5)	flagon (75)
foyer (8)	aerobic (76)
ornithologist (12)	rhythmic (77)
migraine (14)	arugula (79)
porcelain (24)	porringer (80)
capacity (29)	cappuccino (80)
singular (29)	pewter (81)
phenomenon (29)	scorch (81)
mutation (29)	rapturously (83)
camouflaged (29)	satchel (85)
ascertain (30)	battlement (85)
viable (30)	crenellation (86)
lurid (32)	preening (87)
fidget (33)	garnet (89)
Conservatory (33)	topaz (90)
compromise (35)	brooch (90)
geode (47)	retractable (97)
frugal (48)	hunker (98)
thrashing (49)	emitting (103)
frantically (49)	jouncing (103)
lacquer (55)	indignant (112)
elaborate (60)	anemic (115)
gourd (60)	ingested (118)
enquiringly (62)	gizzard (118)
desiccated (66)	rite (122)
hatchling (69)	stifle (130)

Postcards Falcon receives postcards from her father, Peter, from his many worldwide destinations. Have students create a series of New York City postcards (illustrating the places they read about in *Falcon's Egg*, such as the Conservatory Garden or a scene from the Central Park Zoo) and fill them out as though they were Falcon, writing them to Peter.

Graphic organizer: Seasons Comparison
Read aloud the description in which Gray compares spring in the country with spring in New York City (page 33). Have students use a T chart like the one on below to compare each of the seasons in the place they live with that season in Falcon's New York City neighborhood.

Seasons Comparison

Spring Where I Live	Spring in New York City

Home vs. NYC After students have completed the comparison T chart, encourage them to write a persuasive essay in which they support their thesis: "My town/city is a better place to live than New York City," or "New York City is a better place to live than my town/city." Remind them to draw three supporting points from their T chart.

Eggs-traordinary time line Help students sequence the events of *Falcon's Egg* with a time line project. Work with the students to create a time line of *Falcon's Egg*. On the time line, have students place a drawing/painting of Egg each time she makes an appearance in the novel. The time line should end with a large illustration of Egg as she looks when she flies off at the end of the story. Encourage students to take illustration clues from the adjectives Gray uses in her descriptions of Egg.

Journey to Nowhere

Mary Jane Auch

Yearling, 1997

Summary

In the spring of 1815, Remembrance (Mem) Nye accompanies her family on an overland journey from Hartland, Connecticut, to the country in western New York. The trip is an arduous one that only Papa wants to undertake. Mem's strong and rugged spirit serves her well in her many adventures on the trail. Mem, whose heart lies with men's work rather than women's chores, struggles to adjust to the trials of the trip, the tension between her parents, and the isolation and loneliness of her new home.

Background

Mary Jane Auch lives in Ontario, New York, in the Genesee Country, and knows the region well. Her own ancestors settled there in the early nineteenth century. In the early 1800s Genesee Country was home to flocks of settlers who first cleared the heavily timbered land and then developed those rich, fertile lands for farming. The War of 1812 stopped the movement of settlers into New York for a time, and many homesteaders already there abandoned their land and fled. However, shortly after the end of the war, people started to journey to the wilderness again from New England, as Mem's family did.

 **Book Pairing**

You may want to continue reading Mem's story in *Frozen Summer* (Bantam Doubleday Dell, 1998) and *The Road to Home* (Henry Holt, 2000). In *Frozen Summer*, 12-year-old Mem and her family have survived their first Genesee Country winter and now must face the difficulties of Mama's depression and a summer of killing frosts. In *The Road to Home*, Mem is thirteen. Mama is dead, and the farm is a failure. Mem, her father, and her younger brother and sister leave their homestead cabin to return to Connecticut.

Find Out More

About the author Mary Jane Auch is not only a writer but an illustrator as well. You can learn more about her career and her other books by visiting her personal Web site Poultry In Motion: The Books of Mary Jane Auch at **http://www.poultryinmotion.com**.

Genesee Country Students can learn more about this area by visiting the Web site of the Genesee Country Village & Museum in Mumford, New York, at **http://www.gcv.org/**. Be sure to explore the Historic Village links to Homes and Gardens. In addition, articles are reproduced at the site from the Village and Museum newsletter, *The Genesee Country Companion*.

Hands-on Activities

Graphic organizer: Regional Trees (page 26) Help students sharpen their research and classification skills as they complete this organizer. Have them begin by referring to *Journey to Nowhere* to make a list of the trees that grew along the route from Hartland to the Genesee Country. Then have them research and list the trees that are unique to the region in which they live. They can then apply their research and fill in the circles of the Venn diagram.

Map it Have students study the map in the front of *Journey to Nowhere*. Locate a road map of the same states, one that also shows all of the geographic features of the land, and ask students how they might make that same journey today, with our system of roads. See if they can chart a modern-day course by plotting the locations mentioned in each chapter on the map. (If you would like to use the Internet, you can also use Map Quest at **www.mapquest.com** to map the road trip.)

Letters to Grandma Mem, who is Grandma's namesake and shares a special relationship with her, misses Grandma terribly. Have students write an exchange of letters between Mem and Grandma. Help students generate ideas by having them discuss or jot down notes about important events Mem would want to share with Grandma and how Mem felt about them. Then have them imagine how Grandma might reply.

Procedural knowledge The final chapters of *Journey to Nowhere* describe how to build a cabin. Reread these chapters with students and identify this procedural knowledge. Outline the steps required to build a cabin and have students either write them up as a manual for other settlers who will come to Genesee Country, or create a display board of the steps of cabin building.

Field guide to the Eastern Woodlands Mem and her family encounter a variety of Eastern Woodlands animals on the trip and in their new home. Create a class field guide to the animals that they encounter. Have students make a note of the chapter and page number on which each animal is mentioned. Then, in the school library media center, assign students to conduct research on each animal, taking notes on key facts, including physical description, habits and behavior, food, family and young, and habitat and location. Students may also include a picture of the track of each animal Mem might have seen in the woods. Discuss which animals Mem would be likely to encounter today. Why are some of these animals no longer there?

Food for the journey Food wasn't always plentiful or good on the trip to the Genesee Country. But students can research many of these traveling foods on the Internet using a search engine such as **http://www.google.com**. Encourage them to find out about the following foods that the Nyes prepared on their journey or after their arrival. Select one recipe to prepare and share as a class.
journey cake (johnnycake)
cornmeal mush
corn bread
one-two-three-four cake
turtle soup
switchel

Regional Trees
Journey to Nowhere

Trees were an important feature of the landscape for early nineteenth-century settlers. Settlers depended on them for their shelter; they felled and split trees into rough slabs from which they built the first log cabins. Eventually, families hauled felled trees to a nearby sawmill to be cut into boards to build frame houses and barns.

Make a list of the trees that grew along the route from Hartland to the Genesee Country. Then fill in the two circles of the Venn diagram to show which of these trees grew in the Middle Atlantic region at the time of Mem's story and which grow in your region. The area of overlap will show the names of trees that grow in both regions.

Trees Growing in Both Regions

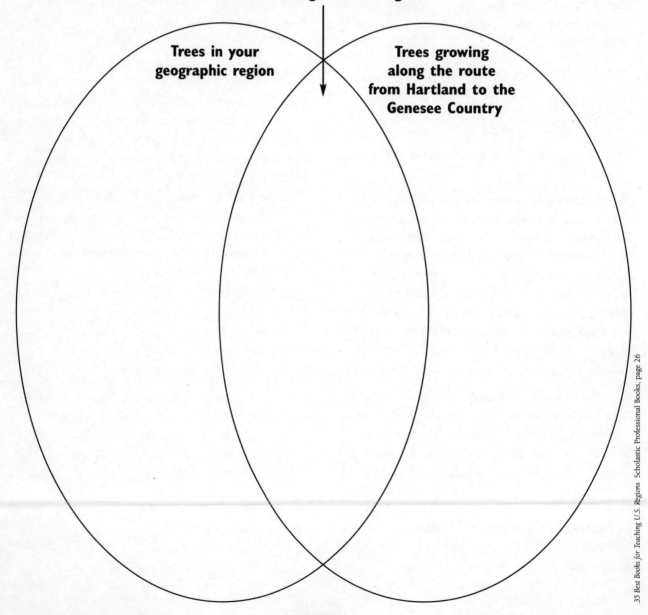

Trees in your geographic region

Trees growing along the route from Hartland to the Genesee Country

 Recorded Books

Homecoming
Cynthia Voigt
Ballantine, 1981

Summary

When Laura Tillerman leaves her four children alone in a car in a Bridgeport, Connecticut, parking lot and walks away, 13-year-old Dicey suddenly becomes the head of the family. She is forced to decide quickly what she and her siblings must do. For weeks, they walk from town to town down the eastern seaboard, heading toward Aunt Cilla's house. What they find there causes them to extend their journey, calling upon a host of survival skills from fishing and clamming to cooking over an open fire and earning money by carrying groceries. The children, under Dicey's devoted leadership, are resourceful and caring, struggling to maintain their identity as individuals and as a family despite the long road home.

Background

Cynthia Voigt says she has had three important jobs in her life: wife-mother, teacher, and writer. She lives in Deer Isle, Maine, now and no longer teaches, but at the time that she was writing *Homecoming*, she lived in Maryland and taught English to second, fifth, and seventh graders at the Key School in Annapolis. The Maryland destination of the Tillerman children was familiar territory to Voigt.

  Book Pairing

Dicey Tillerman's story is continued in the Newbery Award-winning novel *Dicey's Song* (Fawcett, 1983). Voigt thinks of *Dicey's Song* as a continuation of *Homecoming* because it finishes the story that begins in *Homecoming* and tells what happens when the Tillermans get to their grandmother's house and what happens to Mama.

Find Out More

About the author These two sites will provide your students with more biographical information about Cynthia Voigt:

★ Educational Paperback Association "Voigt, Cynthia (1983)" at **http://www.edupaperback. org/pastbios/Voigtcy.html**.

★ Scholastic Author's Online Library "Cynthia Voigt's Biography" at **http://teacher. scholastic.com/authorsandbooks/ authors/voigt/bio.Htm**.

Literature guide For a teacher's guide to *Homecoming*, with emphasis on discussion questions and writing activities, refer to Ballantine Teacher's Guide: *Homecoming* by Arlene M. Pillar at **http://www.randomhouse.com/highschool/ guides/homecoming.html**.

Hands-on Activities

Graphic organizer: Make-a-Metaphor (page 29) Read aloud the excerpted passage in which Dicey compares people to different kinds of boats. Discuss with students how authors often use metaphors to help describe characters and the way those characters behave and think. Then allow students to extend this metaphor by reading more about boats and using this information to make more specific comparisons between boat types and the personalities of the characters in the book and other people they know.

Map it Encourage students to read back through *Homecoming* and track the route the Tillerman children walk from Bridgeport, Connecticut, to Crissfield, Maryland. Students can work from a map of the east coast of the U.S. to trace this route. If they are working with a standard map, students can use a piece of string to outline the route. Have them mark the string where the route begins and ends. Then show them how to straighten out the string and use the map's scale and a ruler to estimate the distance the Tillermans traveled.

Postcards from the Tillermans To accompany the route map they've made, invite students to create illustrated postcards from the stops Dicey and her siblings make along the journey. To make each card, students should review that section of the novel, then write the postcard from the point of view of one of the children.

Tillermans' travels bulletin board Combine the two activities above to create a bulletin board. Post a large map of the eastern seaboard from Cape Cod to Chesapeake Bay. With pins or circle stickers, mark each stop the Tillermans make along their journey. Students can label the key events or people at each location and attach the postcards they've made around the map, using a line of string between the postcard and the appropriate pin or sticker to show at what point in the journey the postcard was written.

Family survey Students come from so many different family configurations. It is beneficial for them to understand that all of these groupings are, indeed, families. In Part Two, Chapter 2, Dicey and James talk about their family and what families are. Work with students to design a survey that they can administer to friends and neighbors. They might want to gather information about people's definitions of family, how many members are in each person's family, who makes the decisions in the family, what makes a family strong, and so on. When each student has surveyed at least three people, review the results as a class. What is the makeup of the families in your survey? What are the most common definitions people gave of family?

Navigating vocabulary When the Tillermans get a ride across the bay in Jerry's sailboat in Part Two, Jerry introduces them to some of the terminology used in sailing. Invite students to explore the language of sailing and sailboats on the Internet. Introduce them to the Think Quest Junior site on Sailing Lingo at **http://tqjunior.thinkquest.org/6169/lingo.htm** or the At Sea site glossary at **http://www.at-sea. cc/glossary/index.shtml**.

Making the food connection: clams Luckily, the Tillerman children were able to fish and dig for clams and mussels along most of their coastal route. What do your students know about clamming? Help them understand more about the way that the Tillermans got their food by having students research clams and the process of clamming. Divide the class into three groups: one to research the clam, one to research clamming, and one to research recipes. If students use the Internet, they'll find a variety of resources on clams and clamming at Foraging.com at **http://www.foraging.com/clamming/**. When their research is complete, have the class vote on several clam recipes, and work with students and parents to prepare a clam lunch.

Make-a-Metaphor
Journey to Nowhere

Metaphors help writers paint a picture with words by comparing two things that are very different, but share some characteristic in common. In Part Two, Chapter 3, Dicey compares people to boats:

> *Maybe life was like a sea, and all the people were like boats. There were big, important yachts and little rafts and motorboats and sailboats and working boats and pleasure boats. And some really big boats like ocean liners or tankers—those would be rich or powerful people, whose lives engulfed many other lives and carried them along.*

Find out more about boats of all shapes, sizes, and uses. Then make a list of 10 to 15 different kinds of boats and consider what kind of "personality" each boat has. Use the graphic organizer below to match people with boats. (If you like, include your classmates' names in the organizer too.)

Person	Characteristic	Type of Boat
Rich or powerful people	Lives engulf other lives and carry them along	Ocean liners Tankers
Dicey		
James		
Maybeth		
Sammy		
Cousin Eunice		
Gram		

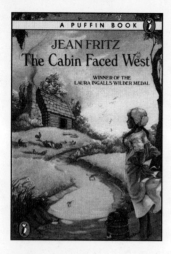

The Cabin Faced West
Jean Fritz
Puffin, 1958

Summary

Just after the end of the Revolutionary War, in 1784, 10-year-old Ann Hamilton and her family move from her beloved Gettysburg, Pennsylvania, across the mountains to the wilderness at Hamilton Hill. Her father and her brothers are especially glad to be settling the new frontier, and her mother is busy with the new baby. Ann, however, misses Gettysburg and the East, and longs for her old life. Throughout the long spring, summer, and early autumn, Ann struggles against her new life and home. It is not until the family has an unexpected visitor that Ann realizes that she is part of something bigger than herself, and that she has come to call Hamilton Hill home.

Background

Jean Fritz was born in Hankow, China. As an only child of American missionary parents, she was often lonely. She did not "come home" to the United States until she was thirteen, and yet Jean Fritz is famous for writing about American history. This is an even stranger choice of subjects given the fact the she didn't like history when she was in school. She hated the way the teachers emphasized dates and wars and left the people out. But Fritz explains that she wanted to know about the people who had lived the history, and that is what she highlights in her historical fiction and nonfiction books.

 Book Pairing

Because *The Cabin Faced West* takes place just after the Revolutionary War, students might be interested in several of Fritz's Revolutionary Era biographies such as *Where Was Patrick Henry on the 29th of May?* (Putnam, 1975), *Why Don't You Get a Horse, Sam Adams?* (Putnam, 1974), *Can't You Make Them Behave, King George?* (Putnam, 1996), *And Then What Happened, Paul Revere?* (Putnam, 1973), *Will You Sign Here, John Hancock?* (Putnam, 1976), and the New Nation title, *Shh! We're Writing the Constitution* (Putnam, 1997).

Find Out More

To learn more about Fritz, visit these Web pages:
★ Carol Hurst's Children's Literature site at **http://www.carolhurst.com/authors/jfritz.html**

★ "Jean Fritz Interview Transcript" at Scholastic's Authors Online Library at **http://teacher.scholastic.com/authorsandbooks/authors/fritz/tscript.htm**

Hands-on Activities

Graphic organizer: A Story from the Past (page 32) Jean Fritz told the story of her ancestors in this novel. Arrange for students to interview an older family member—a grandparent or great-aunt or great-uncle. (If students' relatives are not available, they can interview senior citizens through the local chapter of the AARP.) Brainstorm with students appropriate questions to ask that will bring out some of this person's history. Students might ask their interviewee to describe a time when he or she had a problem or experienced a big change, such as a move. How did the person feel? How did he or she overcome the problem? Encourage students to take notes as they interview, or tape-record the conversation. Have students select one of the stories their interviewee described. With their notes, students can create a plan for this story, using the A Story from the Past map. Students should start by filling in the main characters and the setting, and then identify the kernel of the story (can they summarize it in two sentences?), the main problem, and three major events of the story. Finally, they should fill in the resolution of the story. If they come up with an incomplete section, encourage them to go back to their source and ask about the missing information.

Map it Have students create a map of the journey that the Hamilton family took from Gettysburg, Pennsylvania, to Hamilton Hill (now called Ginger Hill) and that Andy's family takes back to Gettysburg with Uncle John. Encourage students to read closely to find the geographic features that the Hamiltons encountered on the trip and draw and label those features on their route maps.

Ann's diary Ask students to think back to *Journey to Nowhere* (Middle Atlantic section, page 24) in which Mem and her family travel west from Massachusetts to the Genesee Country in New York. Recall the hardships they faced on their journey. Remind students that at her new home on Hamilton Hill, Ann keeps a diary in the book that Margaret gave her when she left Gettysburg. Ask students to think about what Ann might have written in the diary if Fritz had recorded her thoughts about the overland journey with her family. Using the mapping activity above as an entry point, invite students to write three to five journal entries from that trip. How was Ann feeling? What things happened on the trip? How did she feel about the new place when she arrived? Encourage them to include geographic features from the mapping activity in their entries.

After the end . . . Jean Fritz tells us in her Postscript that Ann did really grow up and marry Arthur Scott. Challenge the class to create a group fiction story of how that came to be. Lead the class in story-writing exercises that will generate the necessary story elements. Two of them, of course, are in place—we know the characters and we know the setting. What we do not know are the problems, the solutions, and how the main characters grow and change. If students need additional support, *What's Your Story: A Young Person's Guide to Writing Fiction* by Marion Dane Bauer (Clarion, 1992) is an invaluable guide to helping students write fictional stories.

Design for a church at Hamilton Hill One of the things that David predicted they would do someday at Hamilton Hill was to build a church in the valley. Jean Fritz tells us that her ancestors really did build that church. Work with students to research churches built in the Middle Atlantic U.S. to see what some of them looked like at the end of the eighteenth century. Then have students draw a picture of what they think the Hamilton Hill church might have looked like.

A Story from the Past
The Cabin Faced West

Create a story plan for the story your relative told you. Who are the main characters? What is the setting? What is the kernel of the story? (Give a two-sentence summary.) What is the main problem? Tell the three major events of the story. Finally, state the resolution of the story.

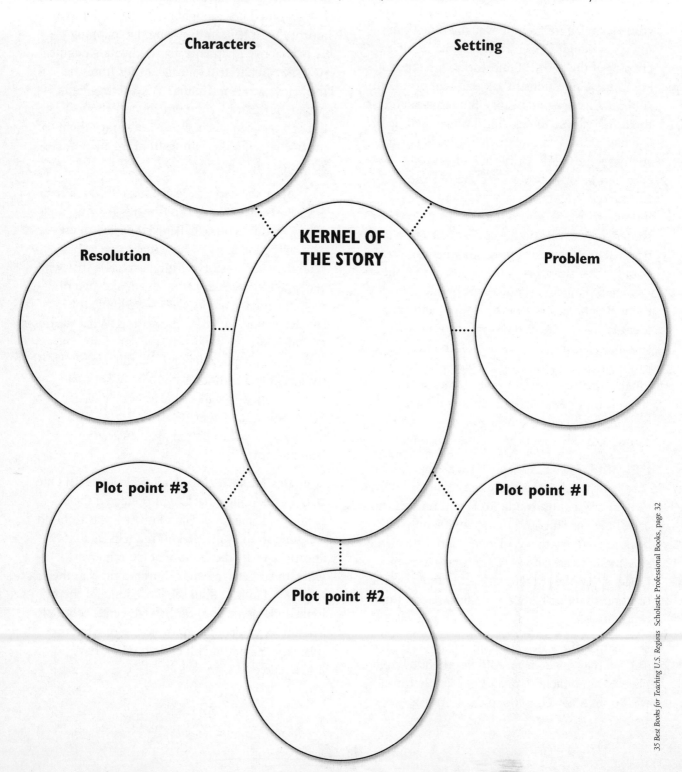

Characters

Setting

Resolution

KERNEL OF THE STORY

Problem

Plot point #3

Plot point #1

Plot point #2

35 Best Books for Teaching U.S. Regions Scholastic Professional Books, page 32

The Day It Rained Forever
Virginia T. Gross

Puffin, 1991

Summary

Christina and her family live above the flood path when the rain comes down for days and the South Fork Dam washes out above Johnstown, Pennsylvania, in 1889, killing thousands of people. On the day of the flood, Christina's brother Frederick leaves for work at the mill in town and her mother is off visiting Uncle Herbert's fiancée in Johnstown. Christina's family has already suffered the loss of their baby a few months before. Now they are frightened that they may lose more family members, this time to the flood.

Background

From the time she was a little girl, Virginia T. Gross tells us in her author's note, her mother told her about the Johnstown Flood. She believed she knew all about it. However, it was not until 100 years after the flood, in 1989, when she read the story of Elsie Frum, a child living north of Johnstown when the flood took place, that she really began to understand the enormity of this natural disaster and to think that there were stories about the flood waiting to be told.

Book Pairing

Author Jane Kurtz lived through a flood herself, the devastating flood of the Red River in Grand Forks, North Dakota, in 1997. Pair her book of narrative poems about that flood, *River Friendly, River Wild* (Simon & Schuster, 2000), with *The Day It Rained Forever.*

Find Out More

The Johnstown Flood The Johnstown Flood National Memorial Park is located in southwestern Pennsylvania, about 19 miles northeast of Johnstown with nearly 165 acres and the remains of the South Fork Dam and portions of the former Lake Conemaugh bed. You can visit the National Park Service Web site at **http://www.nps.gov/jofl/**, call (814)495-4643, or write for further information to:
Superintendent
Johnstown Flood National Memorial
110 Federal Park Road
Gallitzin, PA 16641

Hands-on Activities

 Map it Have students create a map of the Johnstown Flood area, from the South Fork Dam to Johnstown, including the Stony Creek and the Conemaugh River. They'll need to use a detailed state map as a reference.

Chronicle of poems about the flood

After you have read aloud or had students read *River Friendly, River Wild* (see Book Pairing above), assign each student a part in the story of the Johnstown Flood and have them retell that part in a poem. You might begin with a whole-class poem to provide students with a model. To maintain a consistent point of view, students could use Christina as the first-person narrator of their poems. Create a class book of these poems assembled in sequential order, as the events of the story unfold.

Invite a speaker

Invite a meteorologist, or someone from the National Weather Service or the Federal Emergency Management Agency (FEMA) to come to speak to your class about floods. If you live in a region where a different kind of natural disaster is more likely (such as wildfire, earthquakes, hurricanes, or tornadoes), you might find a speaker to come to talk about that topic, for contrast.

And now for a special report . . .

Take the class on a virtual trip to the PBS InFocus: Floods site at **http://www.pbs.org/ newshour/infocus/floods.html** to learn about floods, why they happen, how people survive, and how they save their pets. From the information that students gather, they can create a television news magazine program (like *Dateline*, *20/20*, or *Sixty Minutes*). Invite several teams of students to present a variety of stories about floods in a news magazine format.

Research project and class booklet

In this activity, students research at the library media center the natural disaster that is most likely to happen in their region. Challenge students to learn as much as they can about how the disaster happens and how to stay safe if it does. They can conduct some of their research at the Yahooligans search engine at **http://www. yahooligans.com**. Once students have completed their research, work with them to design a class safety booklet that describes what to do when the disaster strikes.

Letters

To provide students with a current, personal connection to the Johnstown Flood, suggest that they write a letter to someone who has recently experienced a natural disaster. In the newspaper, locate stories about natural disasters happening in the U.S. Select one to read to students (or have them read it) and then have them discuss and write about. Encourage them to compose a letter of support to a survivor in the area they've read about and send their letters to a school in a town near the disaster site. Or they can log on to the Internet and visit the FEMA for Kids site at **http://www.fema.gov/kids/**. There, in "Disaster Connection: Kids to Kids," kids who have been through a disaster can tell their stories with poems, artwork, and essays, and other kids can write cards and letters back to them.

After the flood . . .

The author's note in *The Day It Rained Forever* tells us that nurse Clara Barton arrived five days after the Johnstown Flood and stayed for five months. Have students use a variety of resources, such as *Clara Barton: Civil War Nurse* by Nancy Whitelaw (Enslow, 1997), to research Clara Barton. Once students feel they know the kind of person she was and the work for which she became famous, encourage them to build on their understanding of the Johnstown Flood and write five journal entries that describe Clara Barton's experiences during her Johnstown stay. For background on the flood, students should refer to Christina's story in *The Day It Rained Forever* as well as information at the Johnstown Flood National Memorial site at **http://www.nps.gov/jofl/ home.htm**, which features the full story of the flood, with black-and-white photographs.

Southeast

Featured Regional Readings

★ **West Virginia**
Missing May
by Cynthia Rylant
(Yearling, 1992)

★ **Virginia**
Charley Skedaddle
by Patricia Beatty
(Troll, 1987)

★ **Louisiana**
My Louisiana Sky
by Kimberly Willis Holt
(Yearling, 1998)

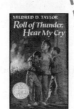

★ **Mississippi**
*Roll of Thunder,
Hear My Cry*
by Mildred D. Taylor
(Puffin, 1976)

★ **Georgia**
Moving Mama to Town
by Ronder Thomas Young
(Yearling, 1997)

Other Recommended Regional Readings

★ **Alabama**
Run Away Home by Patricia McKissack
(Scholastic, 1997)

★ **Florida**
Because of Winn-Dixie by Kate DiCamillo
(Candlewick, 2000)

*The Missing Gator of Gumbo Limbo: An
Ecological Mystery* by Jean Craighead George
(HarperTrophy, 1992)

★ **Georgia**
Be Ever Hopeful, Hannalee by Patricia Beatty
(Troll, 1988)

★ **Kentucky**
Mary on Horseback: Three Mountain Stories by
Rosemary Wells (Viking,1998)

★ **Louisiana**
Melitte by Fatima Shaik (Puffin, 1997)

★ **South Carolina**
The Keeping Room by Anna Myers (Puffin,
1997)

★ **Tennessee**
Clara and the Hoodoo Man by Elizabeth
Partridge (Dutton, 1996)

★ **West Virginia**
Shiloh by Phyllis Reynolds Naylor (Yearling,
1991)

★ **Virginia**
My Brother, My Enemy by Madge Harrah
(Simon & Schuster, 1997)

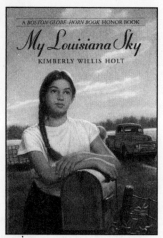

 Listening Library

My Louisiana Sky

Kimberly Willis Holt

Yearling, 1998

Summary

Tiger Ann Parker is happy in Saitter, Louisiana, with her family until the summer of 1957, just after sixth grade, when she is twelve. Suddenly, her world becomes smaller, as she feels herself outgrowing her mentally challenged parents and their limitations. Even Granny can't keep her safe from her feelings of discomfort. But when Granny dies, Tiger is drawn to Aunt Dorie Kay's invitation to leave Saitter and her parents behind for a new life in Baton Rouge. Tiger must struggle with her values, her allegiances, and her own identity as she makes her choice.

Background

The town of Saitter, Louisiana, is fictional, but it is based on the town of Forest Hill, Louisiana, where seven generations of Kimberly Willis Holt's family have lived. On her Web site, Holt tells the inspiration for *My Louisiana Sky*. When she was nine years old, she and her mother were riding down a country road in the Louisiana woods. They passed a woman walking down the road and her mother told her something she never forgot. She said that both the woman and her husband were retarded and that they had many children. That story stayed with Holt throughout her life until, in the 1990s, it became a novel about a girl named Tiger Ann Parker.

 **Book Pairing**

Both Tiger Ann and Aunt Dorie Kay struggle with the intellectual limitations of Tiger's parents. Students might be curious about the role mentally handicapped characters play in two other middle grade novels: *Wish on a Unicorn* by Karen Hesse (Puffin, 1991) and *The Summer of the Swans* by Betsy Byars (Viking, 1970).

Find Out More

About the author Visit the Kimberly Willis Holt Official Website at **http://www.kimberlyholt. com/** to learn more about the author and her books and to find Teacher's Guides to her novels.

Invite a speaker In the Teacher's Guide to *My Louisiana Sky* on Holt's Web site, we learn that there actually was a Hurricane Audrey that brought bad weather to Louisiana in 1957. Invite a meteorologist from the local network television station or the National Weather Service or a professor from a local college or university to speak about hurricanes.

Hands-on Activities

Graphic organizer—Tiger Ann's Choice: Saitter or Baton Rouge? (page 38) Use this comparison matrix to support students as they compare Holt's descriptions of Tiger Ann's life in Saitter with Baton Rouge. Discuss with students how the differences they've generated inform Tiger Ann's decision to leave Saitter.

Map it Have students locate a state map of Louisiana and use it as a model to make their own map that shows the trip Tiger and Aunt Dorie Kay took from Saitter (Forest Hill) to Baton Rouge, marking geographic features along the way.

A new ending . . . Reread the last chapter aloud and pose this question to students: What if Tiger had made the opposite decision about where she would live in the fall? After discussing some of the changes in the plot this turn of events might have created, challenge students to rewrite the chapter from this perspective.

Hurricane watch bulletin board Display a map of the Atlantic seaboard. Select students to take turns as weather watchers and work with them to chart each of the hurricanes in the Atlantic for one season, paying close attention to those that make landfall in Louisiana, as Hurricane Audrey did in *My Louisiana Sky*. Be sure students mark the path and the eventual landfall if the hurricane comes ashore. If you would like to use the Internet, you can visit the Federal Emergency Management Agency (FEMA) Tropical Storm Watch site at **http://www.fema. gov/fema/trop.htm**.

Class weather lore book In Chapter 2, Holt writes about the weather lore that Tiger's Daddy learned from Grandpa Parker. Support students as they research additional weather lore in the library media center and create a class book of weather lore to share. Instruct each student to write and illustrate one page dedicated to a single weather "fact" or "fiction." Gather the pages into a book. If you would like to use the Internet, you can find new weather lore posted each week at the *Old Farmer's Almanac* site by clicking on Weekly Wisdom at **http://www.almanac.com/**. A wonderful read-aloud to pair with this activity is *There Goes Lowell's Party* by Esther Herschenhorn (Holiday, 1998), a lively story of weather fact and fiction.

Tiger Ann's Choice:
Saitter or Baton Rouge?

My Louisiana Sky

Tiger Ann goes to visit Aunt Dorie Kay in Baton Rouge after Granny's death. Use the matrix below to compare Tiger Ann's life with her parents in Saitter with her new life in Baton Rouge. For each category, fill in details you've read about in *My Louisiana Sky*.

Category	Saitter	Baton Rouge
Physical environment		
Family relationships		
Friendships		
Tiger's lifestyle		
Attitudes and beliefs of society		
Tiger's self-image		

 Listening Library

Missing May
Cynthia Rylant

Yearling, 1992

 Book Pairing

When May was nine years old, her family was killed in a flash flood in Ohio. Compare this flood and the way it affected the main character to the flood that takes place in *The Day it Rained Forever* by Virginia T. Gross (Middle Atlantic section, page 33).

Summary

Twelve-year-old orphan Summer has lived with her Aunt May and her Uncle Ob for six happy years when May suddenly dies in her garden. Ob and Summer are bereft at their loss. For six months, with the help of Summer's eccentric classmate, Cletus Underwood, they struggle to pull the fabric of their lives together despite the hole May's absence creates. Finally, they leave their mountainside home in Deep Water, West Virginia, to find a way to contact May and the strength to go on living without her.

Background

Cynthia Rylant was born in Hopewell, Virginia, and by the age of four had moved to live with her grandparents in a house without electricity or running water in the remote West Virginia town of Cool Ridge. They rarely went anywhere because her grandparents had no car. She lived there until she was eight, when her mother finished nursing school. Then she and her mother moved to the southwestern West Virginia town of Beaver. Although Rylant went on to college, earning a degree in library science at Kent State University in Ohio, many of her books, like Missing May, are either set in her home state or are based on her young life in Appalachia.

Find Out More

About the author To learn more about Rylant, visit the Education Paperback Association Web site biography at **http://www.edupaperback. org/authorbios/Rylant_Cynthia.html**.

Literature guides You can find these guides to *Missing May* on the Web:

★ A teaching guide written by Marilyn Joyce on the Information Literacy Projects site at the University of Maine, Department of Computer Science at **http://www.umcs.maine.edu/ ~orono/collaborative/missing.html**.

★ A set of discussion guides for *Missing May* at the Ohio Literacy Resource Center at **http:// literacy.kent.edu/Oasis/Pubs/0300-16.html**.

Whirligigs For background information on whirligigs, visit the Science Museum of Minnesota Web page, "From Windmills to Whirligigs" at **http://www.sci.mus.mn.us/sln/ vollis/index/frontvollis.html**.

Hands-on Activities

Design a whirligig: Two Representations (page 41) Ob designs and builds whirligigs. Some, called "The Mysteries," represent abstract ideas like Love, Dreams, and Death—they are not yard decorations, but art. Talk to students about the difference between concrete art, which represents a figure or scene you can identify, and abstract art, which does not represent things but, like Ob's art, represents ideas and feelings.

Let students explore the difference between these two ways of representing as they work to design two whirligigs that reflect their reading of *Missing May*. Have them use the space to the left on page 41 to design a whirligig that represents a character, object, or scene from the book, such as a landmark from West Virginia. Then have them use the space to the right to design an abstract whirligig that shows an idea or feeling from *Missing May*. (Encourage them to use line, color, texture, and shape to show the idea, rather than to draw a realistic picture.) Extend the exercise by providing students with recycled materials to make their whirligigs three-dimensional or have them design a new cover for *Missing May* in which they incorporate both whirligig designs.

Map it Using a model map of West Virginia and the clues from the story, have students create a route map of the trip that Ob, Summer, and Cletus take from Deep Water to Charleston. Remind students that Glen Meadows is not an actual town. They'll need to put it in a logical spot on their maps. Direct them to Chapters 9 and 10 for clues that will help them decide where Cynthia Rylant intended for Glen Meadows to be.

WV trip plans Invite students to design a travel brochure similar to the AAA guide Ob, Summer, and Cletus consult before their proposed trip to the Spiritualist Church of Glen Meadows in Putnam County and the state capital, Charleston, West Virginia. What sights will students recommend that the characters be sure to see in this state? Have students use the places mentioned in Ob, Summer, and Cletus's travels in *Missing May* and from their own research on West Virginia to design a trifold travel brochure that could be mailed to the characters. For information on West Virginia, refer students to the "Kids Page" at the West Virginia Legislature home page at **http://www.legis.state.wv.us/kids/kids.html**. Read the Activities Book online or download it.

A picture tells a thousand words Cletus collects pictures that tell a story ("Anything with a story to it," he says on page 18) and keeps them in a suitcase. Create a storytelling picture collection file with interesting photographs and/or magazine and newspaper picture clippings. Let each student choose one of the pictures from the collection and write a story to go with it, as Cletus always encourages May to do for his pictures. Encourage them to bring their characters to life the way Cletus does the "Brylcreem guy" in Chapter 13. Students can make a connection to *Missing May* by setting their stories in West Virginia or by using other details from the book. Keep this collection of picture prompts available for students to access during independent writing.

Terrific titles Cletus loves the newspaper title that accompanies the photo of Reverend Miriam B. Young: "The Reverend Miriam B. Young: Small Medium at Large." He tells Ob and Summer, "I'd dearly love to write newspaper titles when I'm grown" (page 52). Give students a chance to play with words and capture the main idea of three favorite pictures from the class picture collection (see activity above). Have them write their clever titles for the pictures on index cards and post all of the titles around the pictures on a bulletin board for classmates to contrast and enjoy.

Design a Whirligig: Two Representations

Missing May

Ob designs and builds whirligigs. His whirligigs, "The Mysteries," are abstract, meaning they show ideas or feelings like Love, Dreams, and Death, rather than people or objects. In the spaces below, design two whirligigs: In the box on the left, draw a whirligig that shows a character, animal, place, or landmark that reminds you most about *Missing May*—your concrete representation. In the box on the right, draw a whirligig that shows an idea or feeling from *Missing May*—your abstract representation.

whirligig—concrete representation: character, animal, place, or landmark	whirligig—abstract representation: an idea or feeling

Moving Mama to Town
Ronder Thomas Young

Yearling, 1997

 Recorded Books

Summary

Freddy James Johnson is thirteen years old in 1947 when his Daddy up and leaves their Georgia farm without a good-bye. When Mama's hired man and new boyfriend, Custis Fullbright, leaves too, Freddy realizes it's time to find a job and an apartment and move his brother Kenneth Lee and his Mama across the state line into town. Freddy makes a go of it, working at Fenton Calhoun's saloon, saving money out of his paycheck each week, and remembering every bit of advice his Daddy ever gave him, until Mama takes it into her head to go back to visit her parents in Saultee, South Carolina.

Background

The humid, subtropical climate of the South unified this region as the great agricultural time was drawing to a close in the 1940s. Freddy's family, like many other rural Southern families, depended on the land for their livelihood—before Daddy left, they could raise enough corn to trade for a new truck. The post-World War II move to increased industrialization, commerce, and big business in the region isn't reflected in this novel, with its hot, sleepy Cole County setting, although the Johnson family's move to town does take them one stop away from the farm and toward a different future.

 **Book Pairing**

Another book about a resourceful young person who takes family problems into her own hands is *A Letter to Mrs. Roosevelt* by C. Coco DeYoung (Delacourte, 1999). In this novel, 11-year-old Margo tries to help her family when the Great Depression threatens them with the loss of their house.

Find Out More

About the author Very little information is available about Ronder Thomas Young, a new author who won an International Reading Association Children's Book Award in 1998. While you may not want to share the article below with students, you will catch a glimpse into her inner character and her capacity to sketch Big Kenny in *Moving Mama to Town* in a way that neither condones nor condemns his behavior. See " 'Recovery' Movement: A Blame Game Carried Too Far" at <u>Unhooked Science Readings</u> at **http://www.unhooked.com/sep/recshame.htm**.

Hands-on Activities

Graphic organizer: Farm Life and Town Life (page 44) Students can use this Venn diagram to compare and contrast Freddy's new life in town to his old life on the farm. Refer them to the book to help generate a list of things that are unique to Freddy's farm life, things that are unique to his town life, and things that are the same. Students can use their completed Venn diagrams to write a persuasive essay that tells which lifestyle they would prefer.

Map it I Cole County, Georgia, and Elderton, South Carolina, are fictional places. However, Young specifically places Freddy's family farm in Georgia, less than an hour over the South Carolina state line. Have students work from regional maps to draw outline maps of Georgia and South Carolina. They can then mark the area in Georgia where the farm might have been located and the area in South Carolina to which the family might have moved. Remind students to use clues from the book to help them, such as the fact that on the return trip home from Saultee, South Carolina, a fictional town near Charleston, it is not out of Susannah's way to go through Columbia.

Map it II Big Kenny told Freddy that a real man "doesn't stick around in the middle of a bad situation." On the first page of the novel, Freddy has a few baskets of peas stashed away. It's not enough to trade for a whole truck, the way Big Kenny traded all of the corn harvest when he left, but Freddy says it's enough for "a good long ride out of here." Using a map of the U.S. and their maps from the activity above as a reference, have students create a road map from the area of Georgia where the farm might have been to Michigan, where Big Kenny is doing factory work. Have students investigate where the biggest industrial city is in Michigan (Detroit) to determine where Big Kenny might be. Then have them trace the route Big Kenny might have traveled.

Class book of truisms Freddy's father, Big Kenny, was a man who sprinkled bits of wisdom about like chicken feed. Big Kenny's sayings appear throughout the book. After a while, Freddy begins to make up his own. Invite students to scan the novel for these truisms and read aloud their favorites. Have students write down and illustrate their favorites on large index cards and then create and illustrate one or two of their own truisms. Compile the truism cards into a classroom book.

Back-in-time bulletin board In 1947, when Freddy posts the barbecue sign for Fenton in Cooper's Drugstore window, he finds the window full of notices and signs that people have hung up for the last ten years. Create a window frame on a bulletin board that would resemble Cooper's Drugstore window, displaying notices and signs from 1937 to 1947. Each student can contribute an advertisement for an event, something for sale, or for a service needed that is related to this time period. Direct students to useful reference books, including *The Century for Young People* by Peter Jennings and Todd Brewster (Doubleday, 1999), *Children's History of the 20th Century* (DK Publishing, 1999), *Timetables of American History* (Touchstone, 1996), or *Timetables of History* by Bernard Grun and Daniel J. Boorstin (Touchstone, 1991).

Farm Life and Town Life

Moving Mama to Town

When Freddy moves his family to town, many things change, while other things remain the same. Can you show the changes, as well as the things that stay the same? In the left circle of the Venn diagram, list as many things as you can that are special about Freddy's farm life. In the right circle, list as many things as you can that are special about his new town life. Then list those things in Freddy's life that remain the same in the overlap area.

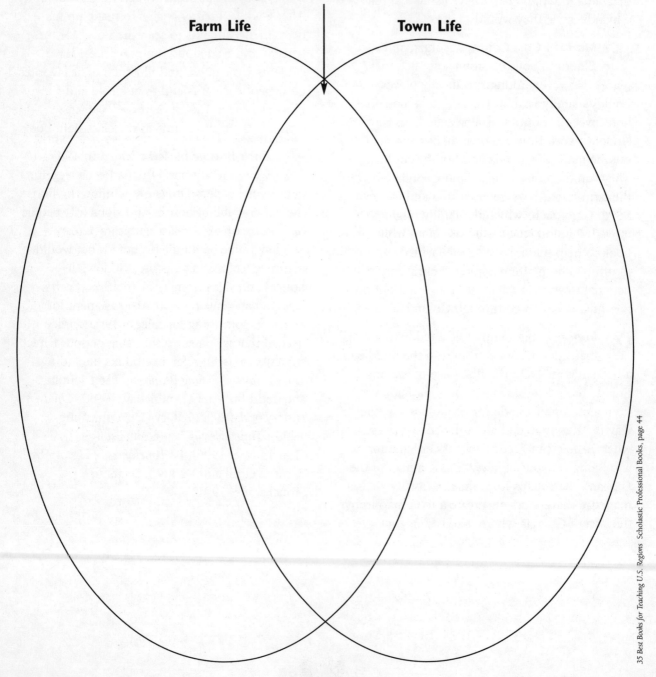

Things that remain the same.

Farm Life   **Town Life**

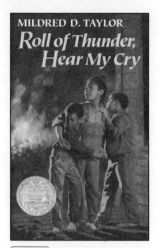

 Recorded Books

Roll of Thunder, Hear My Cry
Mildred D. Taylor

Puffin, 1976

Summary

In 1933, when Cassie Logan is nine, the United States is suffering from the Great Depression. Money is scarce and tempers are short. The Logans, one of the only landowning families in a community of black sharecroppers, must fight alongside all of their neighbors, not only against poverty but also against the racism of whites in the larger rural Mississippi community. Until this point, Cassie has been protected from the prejudice that surrounds her. But this year, she is forced to learn many hard lessons about her worth in the eyes of those who judge by skin color alone.

Background

Although Mildred D. Taylor grew up in Toledo, Ohio, she was born in Jackson, Mississippi, and returned there each summer for family reunions, where she learned the history of her own family and of African-American people. As an adult, she recalled the stories she heard during those summers, stories about the survival of courageous black people in a racist society. In the early seventies, Taylor wrote the first of the Logan stories, *Song of the Trees*, which won first prize in the Council on Interracial Books for Children competition in the African-American category. The book was published in 1975. In 1974, she began to write *Roll of Thunder, Hear My Cry*, which won the 1977 Newbery Medal. Over the years, Taylor has continued to write the Logan family saga. *The Land* (Dial, 2001) is the latest volume.

The breakdown of the plantation system after the Civil War and the emancipation of African-American slaves was the genesis of sharecropping. Sharecropping was a tenant-farming system. Without land of their own, many blacks worked a portion of land owned by whites for a share of the profit from the crops grown. The company store would supply the seeds, equipment, and even food they needed on a tab throughout the year and then settle up once the crops were gathered. Needless to say, at accounting time, the sharecropper was often a few dollars short of what he owed and began the new year with a deficit. This growing deficit, year after year, kept him shackled in a new kind of slavery, in an endless cycle of poverty and life-sapping work. This is why owning their own land was so important to the Logan family.

 Book Pairing

Students' understanding of the history and economic issues involved in the sharecropping in rural Mississippi will enhance their reading of *Roll of Thunder, Hear My Cry*. Two books that can help them learn more about sharecropping are *Osceola: Memories of a Sharecropper's Daughter* by Osceola Mays (Hyperion, 2000) and *Working Cotton* by Sherley Anne Williams (Harcourt, 1992).

Find Out More

About the author To learn more about Mildred D. Taylor, refer to the "Mildred Taylor Teacher Resource File" at the Internet School Library Media Center site at **http://falcon.jmu.edu/~ramseyil/ taylor.html** or the Educational Paperback Association site at **http://www.edupaperback. org/authorbios/Taylor_Mildred.html**.

Literature guide For more teaching ideas, discussion questions, and related activities, see *Literature Guide: Roll of Thunder, Hear My Cry* by Linda Ward Beech (Scholastic, 1998).

Cotton farming Learn more about the history of cotton farming from the time of *Roll of Thunder, Hear My Cry* and how it has changed since then on the homepage of *Cotton Farming* magazine at **http://www.cottonfarming.com/ home/main.html**.

Hands-on Activities

Activity page—Snapshots of Strawberry, Mississippi (page 47) Photographer Ben Shahn took black-and-white photographs of cotton pickers and sharecroppers during a trip through Pulaski County, Arkansas, in the fall of 1935. These photographs will allow students a glimpse into the poverty-stricken lives of the African-American sharecroppers that populate Taylor's novel. Refer students to these photographs, available on the Internet at the American Memory site at **http://memory.loc.gov/ammem/ fsahtml/fachap01.html**. Discuss with the class how these photographs represent the cotton pickers and sharecroppers and what they tell about life for African-Americans living in the South in the 1930s. Lead the discussion back to Cassie's community and the issues of racism and injustice in *Roll of Thunder, Hear My Cry*. In the four frames on this activity page, have students draw images or scenes that Ben Shahn might have photographed if he had visited Strawberry, Mississippi. Students should include a caption for each one, explaining its importance to the story.

Map it The Logan family lived near the fictional town of Strawberry, within driving distance of Vicksburg, Mississippi. Provide students with a regional map and have them locate Vicksburg. Then show them how to use the scale on the map to measure a 75-mile radius around Vicksburg. Ask them what they notice. Students should find that this includes three different states—Mississippi, Louisiana, and Arkansas. Then have them use the same measurement radius on a map that includes their hometown or the nearest large city. Does a 75-mile radius include any other states? Any important bodies of water?

Class poetry book Cassie and her family suffer from prejudice in many ways. Sometimes the most difficult, painful things can be best expressed in poetry, as in the song at the beginning of Chapter 11. Invite students to write a poem about an event from the story from the point of view of one of the Logan family members. Compile a classroom book of students' poetry.

Point-of-view journal entries Jeremy Simms is one of the few whites in the novel who appreciates the Logans and views them as individual people, rather than members of a racial group. The Logan children, though, are often uncomfortable with his friendliness. Assign students to write two journal entries—one from Jeremy's perspective and one from Cassie's about one of the following events in the book: when the school bus narrowly misses running down the Logan children and runs them into the slime of the gully (Chapter 3); when Cassie bumps into Lillian Jean Simms on the street in Strawberry and refuses to step down into the road and offer a second apology (Chapter 5); and when Jeremy brings his Christmas offerings of a bag of nuts for the Logan family and a hand-made flute for Stacey (Chapter 7). Invite students to share their contrasting entries and discuss why Cassie's and Jeremy's perspectives are different.

Snapshots of Strawberry Mississippi

Roll of Thunder, Hear My Cry

Photographer Ben Shahn was hired by the U.S. government to take photographs of cotton pickers and sharecroppers during a trip through Pulaski County, Arkansas, in the fall of 1935. You can see some of these old black-and-white photographs on the Internet at the <u>American Memory</u> site at **http://memory.loc.gov/ammem/fsahtml/fachap01.html**.

Look at these photographs and then think about the story and setting of *Roll of Thunder, Hear My Cry*. Draw four images or scenes that Ben Shahn might have photographed if he had visited Strawberry, Mississippi in 1933 and write a caption for each one, explaining its importance to the story.

caption:

caption:

caption:

caption:

Charley Skedaddle

Patricia Beatty

Troll, 1987

Summary

In 1864, 12-year-old Charley Stephen Quinn is an orphan living in New York City with his grown sister. Following the death of his brother at Gettysburg, he impulsively boards an Army ship headed for the battlefront and becomes a drummer boy in the Civil War. But when he enters his first battle and takes the opportunity to shoot a man, he is overcome with remorse and "skedaddles" (deserts) the army. He makes his way west into the Blue Ridge Mountains, where he lives with a wise woman and learns much about himself, the human race, and the nature of courage.

Background

The Civil War might have been renamed "The Boys' War." While there are no reliable statistics that all authorities agree on, some accounts say that more than two million federal soldiers were under twenty-one, with three hundred or so under thirteen, like Charley, mostly fifers or drummers but regularly enrolled and sometimes serving as fighters. There were places for 40,000 musicians in the Union armies alone. Sometimes the buglers were so small they couldn't climb into saddles without help, yet they rode into battles with their regiments. Figures for Confederate soldiers are even harder to come by, but one sample shows that of 11,000 men only 2,300 were over thirty.

 Book Pairing

The Boys' War: Confederate and Union Soldiers Talk About the Civil War by Jim Murphy (Clarion, 1990) offers firsthand accounts, including diary entries and personal letters, of boys who fought in the Civil War. *Appalachia: The Voices of Sleeping Birds* by Cynthia Rylant (Harcourt, 1991) reveals the way of life in the region of the country known as Appalachia through text and illustration.

Find Out More

About the author Patricia Beatty spent her adult life writing for children, both alone and with John Louis Beatty. You can read more about her inspiring life in the tribute delivered by Judith Auth at the November 1999 Beatty Award Breakfast, California Library Association, November 14, 1999, Palm Springs, California at **http://cla-net.org/groups/beatty/patricia.html**.

Literature guide You will find a literature guide for *Charley Skedaddle* published by Omaha Public Schools, Department of Curriculum and Learning at **http://www.ops.org/curriculum/social-studies/novelguides/charley.html** (from here you can download the full version).

The Civil War These sites provide information and photographs that will help you and your students build background knowledge about this period in American history:

★ <u>Small Planet</u> provides an extensive lesson plan which features *Charley Skedaddle* as well as other middle grade novels at **http://www. smplanet.com/civilwar/civilwar.html**.

★ Selected Civil War photographs from the Library of Congress <u>American Memory</u> site are located at **http://memory.loc.gov/ammem/ cwphtml/cwphome.html**.

★ The <u>American Civil War Homepage</u> maintained by Dr. George H. Hoemann at the University of Tennessee's School of Information Sciences is one of the most extensive Civil War sites on the Internet at **http://sunsite.utk.edu/civil-war/**.

Hands-on Activities

Graphic organizer: Charley's Life in NYC and in the Blue Mountains (page 50) Charley's life and environment in New York City and in the Blue Ridge Mountains are different in every way. Encourage students to use support from the book as they fill out each column of this chart with details that compare the people Charley meets, their values, the environment, his work, and his self-concept in these two very different places.

Map it Provide regional maps that students can refer to as they create a route map of the sea journey that Charley took from New York Harbor to the port city of Alexandria, Virginia, and then the train trip overland to Culpeper, Virginia. Help students build more background by having them mark on this map the Civil War battles that took place during the course of the book in Virginia between 1864 and 1865.

Time line A time line can help anchor students' understanding of chronological events in the plot. Encourage the class to review the book and create a time line of the events of the Civil War during the years 1864 and 1865 as Charley experiences them or hears of them. If students want to use on-line references, direct them to the <u>American Memory</u> Web page "Time Line of the Civil War" at **http://memory.loc.gov/ ammem/cwphtml/tl1864.html**.

Vocabulary exploration The people that Charley encounters in the mountains of Virginia speak a different dialect of English than Charley spoke in New York City. Have students skim through Chapters 8–16 and list the words and phrases that these mountain people use, providing an accompanying definition for each. Remind students to draw their definitions from their understanding of the words in the context of the passages.

Medicinal herbs handbook Granny Bent is a wise woman who knows and uses herbs ("yarbs") to treat people's illnesses. Have students create a medicinal herb handbook that Americans might have used during the Civil War period. Students may include the herbs mentioned in the novel (sassafras, sarsaparilla, and boneset, page 113; pinkroot, spikenard, and pokeweed, page 133; chokecherry and goldenseal, page 153) as well as others they discover in their own research. For each entry, they should draw the plant, explain which part(s) of the plant is used for medicinal purposes, and list the ailments it treats. *The Complete Medicinal Herbal* by Penelope Ody (Dorling Kindersley, 1993), will help students with this assignment or, if you would like to have them use the Internet, students can use the search function at the <u>Medicinal Herbs Online</u> site at **http://www.egregore.com/** to find detailed information on specific herbs.

Charley's Life in NYC and the Blue Ridge Mountains

Charley Skedaddle

Charley's life in New York City is very different from his life in the Blue Ridge Mountains. Fill out the matrix below by drawing comparisons between his life in these two places in each of the following categories: the people Charlie meets, their values and beliefs, the environment, his work, and his self-concept (his image of himself).

Category	Charley's Life in New York City	Charley's Life in Blue Ridge Mountains
People		
Values and beliefs		
Environment		
Work		
Self-concept		

Midwest

Featured Regional Readings

★ **Michigan**
The Watsons Go to Birmingham—1963
by Christopher Paul Curtis
(Yearling, 1995)

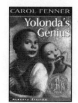

★ **Minnesota**
Moose Tracks
by Mary Casanova
(Scholastic, 1995)

★ **Nebraska**
Prairie Songs
by Pam Conrad
(HarperTrophy, 1985)

★ **Michigan, Illnois**
Yolanda's Genius
by Carol Fenner
(Aladdin, 1995)

★ **Ohio**
The Borning Room
by Paul Fleischman
(HarperTrophy, 1991)

Other Recommended Regional Readings

★ **Indiana**
Running Out of Time by Margaret Peterson
Haddix (Aladdin, 1995)

★ **Iowa**
Addie's Forever Friend by Laurie Lawlor
(Albert Whitman, 1997)

★ **Kansas**
The Van Gogh Café by Cynthia Rylant
(Apple, 1995)

★ **Lake Superior region**
The Birchbark House by Louise Erdrich
(Hyperion, 1999)

★ **Minnesota**
The Winter Room by Gary Paulsen
(Yearling, 1989)

★ **Missouri**
Front Porch Stories at the One-Room School
by Eleanora E. Tate (Yearling, 1992)

★ **Nebraska**
Night of the Twisters by Ivy Ruckman
(HarperTrophy, 1984)

★ **North Dakota**
Jake's Orphan by Peggy Brooke (DK Ink, 2000)

★ **Ohio**
Susannah by Janet Hickman (Greenwillow,
1998)

★ **Wisconsin**
Keeper of the Light by Patricia Curtis Pfitsch
(Simon & Schuster, 1997)

Prairie Songs

Pam Conrad

HarperTrophy, 1985

Summary

Louisa's family is at home with the loneliness of the Nebraska prairie. Certainly they feel the impact of their isolated environment. Doesn't Louisa's mother feel like letting out a long scream after a few days of rain, cooped up with a chattering Louisa in a sod house that drips from the roof? And doesn't everyone mourn the death of the baby who is buried on the prairie? But her family is warm and close. So Louisa is astonished by the new doctor's beautiful wife, who is overwhelmed by "soddie" life, terrified of the possibility that Indians could come to her door, and full of longing for the surroundings, foods, and social life of New York.

Background

Many excellent books show the beauty of the prairies (see the Book Pairing suggestions). In this novel, for Emmeline, the lonely prairie is a terrible place, ultimately a place of madness and death. Frontier life on the prairie was unusually demanding. Tough prairie grasses could not be dislodged, for instance, until adequate plows were invented. A lack of trees on the prairie led to resourcefulness: People burned dried buffalo dung (buffalo chips) and made houses from the earth, using everything they could to beautify their soddies, including quilts.

  Book Pairing

You and your students can look for similarities and differences in several other books that show women having a hard time coping with prairie life, including the novels *Black-eyed Susan* by Jennifer Armstrong (Crown, 1995) and *Bluestem* by Frances Arrington (Philomel, 2000) and the picture book *Dandelions* by Eve Bunting (Harcourt, 1995). Another picture book, *Dakota Dugout* by Ann Turner (Aladdin, 1985), uses poetic, picturesque language to describe life inside a dugout. A recent novel, *Holding Up the Earth* by Dianne E. Gray (Clarion, 2000), uses letters, diaries, and oral history to illustrate the lives of several generations of women on the Nebraska prairie.

Find Out More

Quilting Deborah Hopkinson, author of *Sweet Clara and the Freedom Quilt* (Knopf, 1993), has a Web page with links to many quilting activities at **http://whitman.edu/~hopkinda/**.

Literature guide Carol Hurst's Children's Literature site has links related to Prairie Songs and suggested book connections at **http://www. carolhurst.com/titles/prairiesongs.html**.

Hands-on Activities

✂ **Art activity: story quilt (page 54)** In pioneer times when few families had much extra income, quilts could be made inexpensively. Colorful pieces were made from worn-out clothes, while the backs were sometimes even made from flour sacks. Share some nineteenth-century quilt images with students and then have them think about important setting and character details from *Prairie Songs*. Using the nine-square quilt template students can design a story quilt, using their own illustrations of flora and fauna from the prairie for the corner patches and characters from the novel for the ones in between. They can draw a key scene in the center patch.

🌐 **Map it** Early explorers called the middle section of the United States "the great American desert." Reproduce an outline map of the U.S., and have students use colored pencils to demarcate and show the topography of this part of the continent, which was originally considered impossible for settlement. Discuss with students what changed people's minds about trying to settle the Great Plains.

📈 **City-prairie comparison graphic organizer** Let students create a T chart, like the one below, to compare and contrast Emmeline's life in New York (based on the memories she shares) with her life on the Nebraska prairie. Draw a few comparisons as a class to get them started.

City-Prairie Comparison

Emmeline's life in New York	Emmeline's life on the Prairie
keeps a lovely garden	gathers wildflowers for decoration

💬 **Plains Indians culture presentations** Emmeline is terrified of Indians. Of course, the Plains Indians at that time were also often frightened of the settlers and the changes they brought to Native American life. Divide students into groups to research different aspects of Plains Indian life in the 1800s, including food, transportation, housing, language, clothing, crafts, games and celebrations, adult roles, childhood activities, modern life. A good resource for the group that concentrates on childhood is *A Braid of Lives: Native American Childhood* edited by Neil Philip (Clarion, 2000). It features first-person narratives from many different Native American groups. The group that studies what life is like for the Plains Indians today should read *Grandchildren of the Lakota* by LaVera Rose (Lerner, 1998). Let students figure out interesting ways to present their findings to the rest of the class.

✏ **An interview with Solomon Butcher** In Prairie Songs, Solomon Butcher, an itinerant photographer, takes a picture of Louisa's family. Help students locate Pam Conrad's out-of-print nonfiction book about the real photographer: *Prairie Visions: The Life and Times of Solomon Butcher* by Pam Conrad (HarperTrophy, 1991). Another great resource is *Solomon D. Butcher: Photographing the American Dream* by John E. Carter (University of Nebraska Press, 1986). After students have looked at Butcher's photographs, ask them to imagine that they are reporters who have been asked to interview the photographer. Have them write a list of questions they want to ask about the photographs and about his life. Lead a discussion to elicit students' ideas about what his answers might be.

📖 **How-to guide for prairie construction** It requires procedural knowledge to build a soddie. Have students use a book such as *Zeb, the Cow's On the Roof Again!* by architect Scott Arbuckle (Eakin Press, 1997) to outline the steps required to build one. Suggest that they write the steps as a manual for other settlers who will come to the prairie, or create a display board of the steps of soddie building.

Story Quilt
Prairie Songs

In pioneer times when few families had much extra income, quilts could be made inexpensively. Colorful pieces were made from worn-out clothes, while the backs were sometimes even made from flour sacks. Design a story quilt, using illustrations of flora and fauna from the prairie for the corner patches and characters from the novel for the patches in between. Draw one important scene in the central patch.

Prairie Songs

Yolanda's Genius
Carol Fenner
Aladdin, 1995

Summary

Yolanda loves things passionately: good food, the great Chicago Public Library and Art Institute, her exuberant aunt Tiny, and her little brother Andrew. When a school shooting and a drug encounter convince Yolanda's mother to move her family to the quiet town of Grand River, Michigan, Yolanda has some educating to do. With confidence and aplomb, she stands up to her classmates when they tease her about her vocabulary and her weight, some tough skateboarders who crush her brother's harmonica, and the music store owner, who agrees to mark down a harmonica for a musical genius. But how can she let a whole blues festival know that Andrew is not just a quiet little boy but a musical genius?

Background

Carol Fenner says, "Long before I went to school, I decided I would be a poet. I remember sitting in a vast field of grass and sun and dandelions and being filled with such an excess of pleasure and happiness that I couldn't contain it." Fenner—who grew up in a house filled with books and stories read aloud—gives her character Yolanda this same love of words. Her husband's passion for listening to live music led her to a jazz festival in Chicago where a "lost child" (who looked anything but lost) was brought on stage, sparking the idea for *Yolanda's Genius*.

Book Pairing

Among the most compelling parts of this Newbery Honor Book are the passages that make the reader "feel music." *Yolanda's Genius* can be paired with any number of books that celebrate music, including Newbery Award-winning novel, *Bud, Not Buddy* (Delacorte, 1999), which offers passages that are striking in their ability to capture music in words. Two poetic picture books that compliment *Yolanda's Genius* are *Harlem: A Poem* by Walter Dean Myers (Scholastic, 1997) and *I See the Rhythm* by Toyomi Igus (Children's Press, 1998).

Find Out More

Literature link Visit Yolanda's Genius at **http://www.eduscapes.com/newbery/96d.html** for a number of links to related pages such as "B. B. King, King of the Blues," "What is a Paralegal?" and a list of blues bands.

Chicago Students can see more of what Yolanda loves about Chicago at the following sites:

★ The Art Institute of Chicago at **http://www.artic.edu/**

★ "Museums and Zoos in Chicago, Illinois" on the Family Travel site at **http://www.familytravelguides.com/articles/museums/m&z9.html**

Hands-on Activities

Graphic organizer: Rural and Urban Life—Then and Now (page 57) Ask students to consider what's different about life in the city and life in the country based on their own experiences and what they've learned in *Yolanda's Genius* about Chicago versus Grand River. Have them fill in details about public buildings, housing, problems, and reformers in the rural-urban 1990s comparison section. For the early twentieth century comparison, refer students to *Turn of the Century: Our Nation One Hundred Years Ago* by Nancy Smiler Levinson (Lodestar, 1994).

Map it Use a city map to find all Chicago landmarks mentioned in the novel, including Lake Shore Drive, Museum of Science and Industry, Soldier's Field, Lake Michigan, Shedd Aquarium, Public Library, Art Institute, Grant Park, skyline, Saks Fifth Avenue, Rush Street, Neiman, Water Tower, Michigan Avenue, East Jackson, Columbus Drive, and Petrillo Music Shell. Direct students to **http://www.ci.chi.il. us/tourism/** to find an interactive map with pictures on the City of Chicago site. They can also call 1-800-226-6632 for a copy of the Chicago Official Visitor's Guide.

Yolanda's word list Yolanda is fascinated by the dictionary. Create a class dictionary with some or all of the following words from *Yolanda's Genius*. Make sure students consult a real dictionary to check their definitions and, if you want, to provide other entry information, such as pronunciation, word origin, part of speech, and so forth. Tell students that some of these words can't be found in a dictionary, so it's up to them, the dictionary writers, to figure out good definitions based on the context of the passage in which they find the words.

junkie (1)
pushers (3)
sniggering (13)
blisterface (15)
dirgelike (16)
jocks (27)

gravelly (42)
sobered (44)
jmincing (47)
haphazard (54)
vortex (59)
scuttled (64)
henchmen (65, 109)
listlessly (72)
sluiced (86)
blues harps (87)
vengeance (94)
thwacking (95)
mirth (98)
demurely (98)
opulent (110)
entrepreneur (110)
simmered (121)
palisades (130)
sedately (133)
know-nuthin' (134)
ravishing (140)
gummy (147)
cacophony (159)
yuppie (160)
shenille (161)
tempura (162)
mojo (183)
tumult (184)
anguish (188)
audiating (194)

Do you double Dutch? The jump rope game double Dutch plays a big part in *Yolanda's Genius*. This is a wonderful rhythm-enhancing and coordination-building activity to teach students to play on the playground. If you don't know how to play, check out *The Jump Rope Book* by Elizabeth Loredo (Workman, 2000).

How-to guide Build on the activity above by challenging students to create a how-to guide that includes descriptions of what it's like to play double Dutch, the rules (students may wish to include variations of rules), and rhymes that go with the jumping. Students might enjoy contacting students in another region of the U.S. to learn about double Dutch customs from other places to include in their book.

Read all about it! Have students imagine that they are reporters assigned to write a newspaper story about the blues concert on the day that Yolanda and her little brother happen to pop up on stage. Ask students to write down notes about the 5 W's (who, what, when, where, and why) and compose a compelling lead paragraph that grabs the reader's attention. They can continue their stories from there.

Rural and Urban Life—Then and Now
Yolanda's Genius

Yolanda and her family move from urban Chicago to rural Grand River, Michigan, and spend much of the rest of the book comparing the two! What's different about life in the city from life in the country? Think about what you learned in *Yolanda's Genius* about Chicago and Grand River for the 1990s comparison. For the other, use *Turn of the Century: Our Nation One Hundred Years Ago* by Nancy Smiler Levinson (Lodestar, 1994), which will help you understand what the city of Chicago was like at the turn of the century.

Rural–Early Twentieth Century	Urban–Early Twentieth Century
public buildings	**public buildings**
housing	**housing**
problems	**problems**
reformers	**reformers**

Rural–1990s	Urban–1990s
public buildings	**public buildings**
housing	**housing**
problems	**problems**
reformers	**reformers**

Moose Tracks
Mary Casanova
Scholastic, 1995

Summary

Seth's stepfather is a game warden in the Minnesota north woods, so Seth knows all about responsible hunting versus poaching. Nevertheless, Seth can't resist sneaking his shotgun out of the house to kill his first rabbit. The next day, while out on his horse, he returns to the woods to check out some moose tracks and stumbles onto poachers killing a moose cow. Although the poachers threaten to harm Seth and his family if Seth doesn't stay away, he knows he has to try to save the orphaned moose calf.

Background

Like Seth, the author's grandfather was once treed by a moose on a cold, wintry day. She says, "My grandpa's story, along with my own fascination with these lanky and magnificent animals, became the initial inspiration for writing *Moose Tracks*, my first novel. I drew also on newspaper accounts of individuals who had been arrested for poaching here on the Minnesota-Canadian border. In writing *Moose Tracks*, I wanted to share my love for the wilderness, and at the same time (coming from a hunting family with seven brothers), I wanted to explore the differences between poaching and responsible hunting, namely, the ethics of taking an animal's life."

Book Pairing

Mary Casanova's *Wolf Shadows* (Hyperion, 1999), a sequel to *Moose Track*, tackles more of the complex issues that arise when people and animals share the land. Students will have a chance once again to see Seth confront ethical issues and his own fears.

Find Out More

Author connection Read about Mary Casanova's own encounters with moose on her Web page at **http://www.marycasanova.com**. You can print out a display of her other book covers that are connected with the Minnesota north woods to generate student interest.

Moose These sites can help you and your students make a connection with these fascinating creatures:

★ The Great North Woods site at **http://www. greatnorthwoods.org/moose/** has many pictures of moose, including ones in accidents with human beings.

★ Find more great pictures and facts on the "Moose" page at **http://eduscapes.com/nature/ moose/kids.htm**.

Hands-on Activities

Graphic organizer: Collecting Cool Animal and Plant Facts—A Field Guide
Encourage students to find out about the natural resources from the Midwest region of the U.S. mentioned in *Moose Tracks*, including moose, rabbit, aspen, birch, sumac, maple, moss-covered forest floor, wild rice lakes, Norway pines, white pine, partridge, black bear, winter ticks, porcupine, red fox, deer, peat bog, tamarack, cattails, pumpkins, chickadee, cedar, ravens, sparrows, stream, wolf, lynx, beaver, otter, marten, mink, wolf spider. Have students use the book to fill in information about the animals and plants they have read about, making a note of any description the author provides and the page(s) on which the natural resource is mentioned.

Map it In the book, the county map shows that nearly all the land beyond Seth's house belongs to the state (page 98). Have students compare a county map and a state map. Which features are similar? Which features are different? Minnesota maps can be ordered from the Hudson Map Company (1-800-473-1412). Find maps on the Internet at TopoZone.com at **http://www.topozone.com** (type "Koochiching County" into the place finder).

Tracks on the Internet Students can observe the tracks of different species by visiting the National Wildlife Federation "Games Page" at **http://www.nwf.org/kids/games.html** and playing the animal tracks matching game. Then have them research the actual size and shape of moose tracks. Using rulers, pencils, craft paper, and scissors to design actual-size moose hoofprints, have students create a "moose tracks" path to your classroom or to the library media center.

Moose bulletin board Assign students to gather facts about moose. They can find out what moose eat, how big they are, what a "moose wallow" and a "rut" are, how long moose live, how big moose calves are, what natural dangers moose face, and more. When they have collected all of their facts, have students write the facts on index cards and illustrate them. Post the illustrations and related facts on a Moose bulletin board under categories such as food, habitat, life facts, and so forth.

Will they do the right thing? Seth shoots a wild rabbit for its paw, partly out of peer pressure from his friend Matt and partly as an attempt to prove his "bravery" to his stepfather. Later, when Seth sees what the poachers have done, he must think more closely about his own actions. Lead a discussion with students about ethical decisions and choices they think many of their peers at school face. Record their ideas on the board or on chart paper and let them pick one issue of interest. Have students write two or three journal entries from the point of view of a person who faces a difficult decision about the chosen topic and who tries to figure out the right choice and next steps. If students feel comfortable, let them share their entries and discuss whether their characters made ethical choices.

Persuasive essay: hunting Mary Casanova says that she drew her story's theme from the Ojibwa in the northern Minnesota region who believe that all life is a gift to be treated with respect and that humility is at the heart of true strength. The Ojibwa were known to thank an animal for giving its life. Seth does something similar near the end of *Moose Tracks*. Lucy in *The Ballad of Lucy Whipple* (see Pacific section, page 101) also tries that approach with the squirrels, rabbits, and prairie chickens she shoots for her family's dinner. Ask students how Lucy's and Seth's attitudes about hunting differ, and how they are similar. After discussing various attitudes about hunting, encourage students to voice their own opinions by writing a persuasive essay in support of or against hunting, constructing support for the position they take.

Collecting Cool Animal and Plant Facts—A Field Guide

Moose Tracks

Find out about the natural resources from the Midwest region of the U.S. mentioned in *Moose Tracks*, including moose, rabbit, aspen, birch, sumac, maple, moss-covered forest floor, wild rice lakes, Norway pines, white pine, partridge, black bear, winter ticks, porcupine, red fox, deer, peat bog, tamarack, cattails, pumpkins, chickadee, cedar, ravens, sparrows, stream, wolf, lynx, beaver, otter, marten, mink, wolf spider. Fill in this chart, making a note of any description the author provides and the page(s) on which the natural resource is mentioned.

Mammal	Bird	Insect	Plant
			Aspen, birch, maple leaves— decaying, p. 3

Now make your own *Moose Tracks* animal/plant fact cards. Use one index card for each of the spaces you have filled in the chart above. On these index cards collect information you find about the animals and plants. When you've finished researching, sort your cards by the categories listed above. Write the information you've collected as entries for a field guide. Be sure to include illustrations and all the essential facts: physical description, habitat, location and (for the animals) food and habits, and other fascinating facts. If possible, draw a picture of the track of each animal Seth might see in the woods.

 Recorded Books

The Watsons Go to Birmingham–1963
Christopher Paul Curtis
Yearling, 1995

Summary

Ten-year-old Kenny is thrilled to be in a 1948 Plymouth headed to Birmingham, Alabama, where his momma grew up. He likes to be around Dad, who will "cut up" the minute he thinks he can get the family laughing; he gets to take a long trip in the Brown Bomber with its new record player; and he's going to deliver his 13-year-old brother (who has become an "official juvenile delinquent") to Grandma in Alabama to get straightened out. What Kenny doesn't know is that the trip will land his family in Birmingham just in time to be part of a terrible moment in history.

Background

Christopher Paul Curtis was working in a factory in Flint, Michigan, when he first began to think of himself as a writer. He and another 18-year-old made a deal to double-up shifts, so they would each have 30 minutes at a time off the line. Curtis used his time to write. Years later, when his wife suggested that he take a year off factory work to focus on his fiction, *The Watsons Go to Birmingham—1963* was born, to great applause. A second novel, *Bud, Not Buddy* (Delacorte, 1999), won both the Coretta Scott King Award for fiction and the Newbery Award in 1999.

A note to consider if you read this novel out loud: Curtis is right on target with the sometimes casual cruelty of kids toward other kids—especially through his characterization of Kenny's older brother, Byron. At the same time, Curtis reveals a tight bond between the Watson siblings in subtle ways. As you read, you may want to discuss this issue and also guide the class to look for hints that Byron is really soft-hearted.

Book Pairing

Dad tells the family that he used to work in a barbershop. Read the picture book *Uncle Jed's Barbershop* by Margaree King Mitchell (Aladdin, 1993) and discuss how different Dad's experience would have been in Michigan compared to Uncle Ned's in the segregated South.

Find Out More

About the author A good Web page, "Christopher Paul Curtis Teacher Resource," can be found at the Internet School Library Media Center site at **http://falcon.jmu.edu/~ramseyil/curtis.htm**.

Literature guide A Web page with a message from the author, a prereading activity, thematic connections, and Internet resources can be found at RandomHouse.com at **http://www.random house. com/teachers/guides/wats.html**.

Hands-on Activities

Map it Challenge students to create a map of the trip the Watsons take from Flint to Birmingham on I-75, the highway that Kenny boasts "runs all the way from Flint to Florida." Use state road maps to follow the highway route.

Cross-country trip planning Momma creates a notebook where she figures out the mileage and all the food and stops. Invite students to plan a cross-country road trip to a city of their choice and prepare a notebook like Momma's for a trip they want to take. Students can calculate how many miles they will need to travel and estimate how many days their trip will take. Have them separate their travel notebook by days and include a budget for food and gas, as well as notes on the highways they plan to use, the landmarks they want to see, and the places they may want to drive through.

The '60s presentation Divide students into groups to research things mentioned in the novel that help show daily life in 1963: the record player in the car, "Yakety Yak" and other songs, the "conk" hairstyle, Buster Brown shoes, and "Felix the Cat" and other cartoons from that era. Students' best source of information may be interviews with people who were adults during the 1960s. Time Life's *This Fabulous Century: The 1960s* is another great resource. Students can present their findings in a "Back to the '60s" documentary-style presentation.

Dig that vocabulary Christopher Paul Curtis carefully suggests his 1960s setting through the use of popular expressions (such as *conk, Daddy-O,* and *dig this*) and other references to popular culture. Invite students to create a glossary for the novel, drawing their definitions from the text surrounding the words and from the group presentations.

Civil rights research What can students find out about the actual church bombing Christopher Paul Curtis weaves into his plot?

(To begin, read with students the information about the civil rights movement in the Afterword.) Martin Luther King, Jr. spoke at the funeral of three of the girls killed in the bombing and talked about life being "as hard as crucible steel." If students use the Internet, direct them to "We Shall Overcome: Historic Places of the Civil Rights Movement" at **http://www.cr.nps.gov/nr/travel/civilrights/**. Click on "List of Sites" and then on "Sixteenth St. Baptist Church" to see a picture of the church and read about the church bombing. Have students share what they've learned to gain a deeper understanding of the history of this tragedy.

Flint versus Birmingham Use a T chart to help students compare and contrast Flint, Michigan, with Birmingham, Alabama, in the middle of the twentieth century, focusing on the lives of African Americans in the South and the North. Have students contribute ideas, using the comments that members of the Watson family make to support their observations of these differences.

Lives of African Americans Living in Flint, Michigan— the North (1963)	Lives of African Americans Living in Alabama— the South (1963)

The moral of the story is . . . Byron tells Kenny, "But you just gotta understand that that's the way it is and keep on steppin'." Let students discuss what they think Byron means and then have them visit "Aesop's Fables Online Collection" at **www.pacificnet.net/~johnr/aesop/** and try to find a fable or fables that make the same point.

Bryron, a.k.a. Narcissus Invite students to read the legend of Narcissus (mentioned on page 15) and make two sets of dioramas—one set that illustrates the legend and another set that illustrates scenes in the novel that show Byron acting as Narcissus did.

The Borning Room
Paul Fleischman

HarperTrophy, 1991

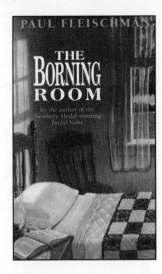

Summary

Georgina Caroline Lott sits in the room where she was born and tells the story of her life—all the births and deaths and near deaths that happened in that "borning room." When she is eight, she helps a runaway slave who, in turn, helps Georgina's mother give birth to a son, Zeb. When she is twelve, she walks in the woods with her free-thinking grandfather and then sits with him as he dies. When she is fourteen, her mother dies in childbirth. Two years later, with the help of the new schoolteacher, she manages to save Zeb from diphtheria. In the last chapter, it becomes clear that she, herself, is now an old woman about to die, thinking about the past but also about her grandchildren, the future.

Background

In 1987, Sid Fleischman won the Newbery Award for his novel *The Whipping Boy*. Two years later, his son, Paul Fleischman, was also awarded a Newbery Medal—for *Joyful Noise*, a book of poetry celebrating the world of insects. The natural world and a rich, literary vocabulary show up in Paul Fleischman's books again and again. *The Borning Room* is no exception. This fairly slow-moving novel—one review journal called it "a quiet cycle of episodes"—is rich in allusions to historical events, using one woman's life to illuminate the dramatic changes that can happen in one lifetime, in medicine, social customs, fashions, and so on.

Depending on your students' backgrounds, you may decide the best approach is to do quite a bit of background work—introducing them to the music of Beethoven, Schubert, and Haydn, and the words of Dickens, Wordsworth, Coleridge, and Keats, for instance. You can also use the novel as a good opportunity to see how much students can deduce from clues. On page 33, for instance, Georgina's mother notes that they have delivered a woman from slavery and must continue with that work. "That night, as Mama instructed," Georgina says, "I lit a lamp, then hung it in the garret window." Can students guess that Georgina's family has decided to become a stop on the Underground Railroad? On page 40, Georgina says, "All the talk was of the war. Two Beeton boys had just died at Vicksburg." Can students tell that she is talking about what we now call the Civil War?

If you have time, you may want to create research projects such as tracking down the words to songs ("John Brown's Body" and "Three Hundred Thousand More," for example) or organize class presentations on such things as rag dolls, corn husk dolls, and bustles.

Book Pairing

Since the borning room is a place of birth and death, this may be a time to talk about death and bring in some of the many good picture books that discuss grieving and how people go on after death. *Pulling the Lion's Tail* by Jane Kurtz (Simon & Schuster, 1996) is one example.

Find Out More

About the author An author page about Paul Fleischman with biographical data and an e-mail link is available at **http://www.people.virginia. edu/~lbs5z/PPointPF/**.

Literature guide The Omaha Public Schools Novel Guide site provides information about *The Borning Room* and related links at **http://www. ops.org/curriculum/social-studies/ novelguides/borning.html**.

A borning room You can read about a borning room in a real historical house at **http://www. alden.org/museum/houstour/borningroom. htm** from Alden House Museum Virtual Tour Borning Room.

The Underground Railroad Help students locate these resources as they research the Underground Railroad:

Dear Austin: Letters from the Underground Railroad by Elvira Woodruff (Knopf, 1998)

Bright Freedom's Song: A Story of the Underground Railroad by Gloria Houston (Harcourt, 1998)

Escape from Slavery: Five Journeys to Freedom by Doreen Rappaport (HarperCollins, 1991)

Minty: A Story of Young Harriet Tubman by Alan Schroeder (Dial, 1996)

Bound for the North Star: True Stories of Fugitive Slaves by Dennis Brindell Fradin (Clarion, 2000) (archival prints and photographs)

Hands-on Activities

Map it In 1800s America, many families moved again and again, always heading to a new frontier. Have students find information in the novel and use a map to locate the route Georgina's family took to get to Ohio.

Underground Railroad route maps Georgina says, "I knew there was slavery just across the Ohio and had heard of the Underground Railroad, but I'd never set eyes on a runaway" (page 12). *Sweet Clara and the Freedom Quilt* by Deborah Hopkinson (Knopf, 1993) explains one way escaping slaves managed to put maps together. Students can use the map in *The Underground Railroad* by Raymond Bial (Houghton Mifflin, 1995), which can also be found at Underground Railroad Routes 1860 **http://education.ucdavis.edu/NEW/STC/ lesson/socstud/railroad/map.htm**, to draw one route that an escaping slave might take to freedom.

Handshakes and history Hands play an important part in *The Borning Room*. For example, we learn that Grandfather shook Ben Franklin's hand when Grandfather was five. Read aloud to students *Pink and Say* by Patricia Polacco (Philomel, 1994) to learn more about another memorable handshake and a special friendship between two boys during the Civil War. Then encourage them to draw the scenes from both *Pink and Say* and *The Borning Room* that mention hands. You can create a display to show the scenes students have drawn.

Cover design On the first page of *The Borning Room*, the narrator talks about the sugar maple cherished by her grandfather. The reader sees that maple from time to time throughout the novel. When Zeb is deathly sick, for example, Georgina hears the wind moaning in the maple and thinks that her family is "becoming a leafless tree" (page 86). Have

students research maple trees so that they can draw an accurate picture of one. Then invite them to design a new cover for *The Borning Room* that incorporates a maple tree.

Aphorisms and famous quotations

Grandfather is fond of Ben Franklin's sayings (aphorisms), such as, "Three may keep a secret if two of them are dead" (page 23). Have students make an illustrated class booklet using the Ben Franklin sayings they can find in *The Borning Room* and in other sources. Refer them to *Bartlett's Quotations* or direct them to <u>Bartleby.com</u> at **http://www.bartleby.com/100/**, where they can follow the link to <u>Bartlett's Quotations</u> and type in "Benjamin Franklin." You can also buy a copy of *Wit and Wisdom from Poor Richard's Almanack* by Benjamin Franklin (Dover Publications, 1999) for $1.00.

Picturing people before photography

Before photography, as Fleischman describes on page 38 of *The Borning Room*, a silhouette was often the only image a person had of an ancestor. In the novel, the next type of image mentioned is a painting: Mama finds a portrait painter "that Grandfather might be painted before he died" (page 48). Still later, Mr. Snell takes photographs (page 85). To help students get a sense of how different generations could see their ancestors, have students work in pairs. Invite each student to create three different pictures of his or her partner: a silhouette (they might use an overhead projector to cast a shadow of and trace around their partner's head), a painting or drawing, and a photograph. Compare the results.

Time line

Many different inventions that appeared during Georgina Carolina Lott's lifetime, from 1851 to 1918, are mentioned, including the telegraph, railroads, sewing machines, the McCormick reaper, chloroform, automobiles, telephones, and electric lights. Have students list all of the different inventions with the page numbers where they are mentioned and then work from that list to make a time line of Georgina Carolina Lott's life, showing when each invention appeared.

Southwest

Featured Regional Readings

★ **Oklahoma**
Out of the Dust
by Karen Hesse
(Scholastic, 1998)

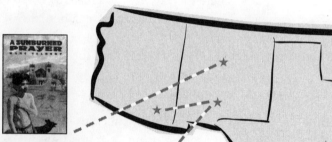

★ **New Mexico**
A Sunburned Prayer
by Marc Talbert
(Aladdin, 1995)

★ **Arizona,
New Mexico**
Sing Down the Moon
by Scott O'Dell
(Yearling, 1996)

★ **Texas**
*Search for the
Shadowman*
by Joan Lowery
Nixon
(Yearling, 1996)

★ **Missouri, Texas,
Tennessee**
*Justin and the Best
Biscuits in the World*
by Mildred Pitts
Walter
(Knopf, 1986)

Other Recommended Regional Readings

★ **Arizona, California**
If That Breathes Fire, We're Toast! by Jennifer J. Stewart (Holiday House, 1999)

★ **New Mexico**
And Now Miguel by Joseph Krumgold (HarperTrophy, 1953)

Kokopelli's Flute by Will Hobbs (Camelot, 1995)

★ **Oklahoma**
Red-Dirt Jessie by Anna Myers (Walker, 1994)

★ **Texas**
Canyons by Gary Paulsen (Laurel Leaf, 1990)

Holes by Louis Sachar (Yearling, 1998)

Old Yeller by Fred Gipson (Harper Trophy, 1956)

White Lilacs by Carolyn Meyer (Harcourt, 1993)

★ **Southwest—general**
Canto Familiar by Gary Soto (Harcourt, 1995)

Words by Heart by Ouida Sebestyen (Yearling, 1979)

Out of the Dust

Karen Hesse

Scholastic, 1998

🔊 **Listening Library**

Summary

Fourteen-year-old Billie Jo Kelby's voice speaks powerfully out of the free-verse poems that make up this novel—telling of pregnant Ma who says only "I knew you could" when Billie gets the highest achievement test score in the eighth grade; of Billie's friends who encourage her to play sizzling hot piano pieces; of Daddy who is rooted to the land and will fight the dust until he has to sit coughing and spitting mud. Into this tough life comes horror when Daddy leaves a pail of kerosene next to the stove and Billie accidentally sets her mother on fire. How can anyone survive this kind of sorrow, "big as Texas"?

Background

During the Great Depression, dust blew for seven years, turning more than 100 counties in Kansas, Oklahoma, Colorado, New Mexico, and Texas into what is now known as the Dust Bowl. Families did everything they could to keep the dust from their houses, but they ended up living with dust night and day—eating their food mixed with grit, putting wet cloths over their mouths to sleep. Karen Hesse was working on the picture book *Come On, Rain* (Scholastic, 1999) when she became captivated by photographs and news accounts of the "dirty thirties"

and ended up writing *Out of the Dust*, her Newbery Award–winning novel.

 Book Pairing

Actual stories of some Dust Bowl children— drawn from written documents and interviews and illustrated with photographs— are documented in *Children of the Dust Bowl: The True Story of the School at Weedpatch Camp* by Jerry Stanley. To give students a perspective on how Billie Jo's story might have changed if she had made it to California, encourage students to read *Cat Running* by Zilpha Keatley Snyder, the story of a girl in California who is upset when she thinks her life has been invaded by "Okies."

Find Out More

The Dust Bowl A good book for background is *Driven from the Land: The Story of the Dust Bowl* by Milton Meltzer (Marshall Cavendish, 2000), which includes a map, photographs, a song, and many stories.

Literature guide A novel study page by author and educator Annette Lamb, with links, is available at the Eduscape site's "Out of the Dust" page a **http://eduscapes.com/newbery/98a.html**.

Author readings The Riverdale School District site at **http://www.riverdale.k12.or.us/ ~cmaxwell/dust.htm** features the author reading excerpts from *Out of the Dust*.

Hands-on Activities

✂ **Art activity: Key Scenes by Season (page 69)** Ask students to explain how this book is organized. They should notice that Billie Jo divides her story into six seasons, and that the events, the weather, and the mood are connected with each season's characteristics. For each of the seasons listed on the Key Scenes by Season page, have students decide on the most important scene from that section and draw it in the middle of the box. Around each picture, encourage students to use symbols and color to show what the weather is doing around Billie Jo. When students finish their drawings, encourage them to compare their ideas. Did everyone choose the same key scene and can the class agree on a key scene to stand for that section?

Map it Build geographic background for *Out of the Dust* by finding a map in a reference book, such as the *World Book Encyclopedia*, that shows the area affected by the Dust Bowl. Have students trace the area of the Dust Bowl on U.S. outline maps. Note that while Billie Jo lives on a farm in a rural area, several nearby towns and rivers are mentioned (see pages 17, 67, 70, 103, 125, 129, 163, and 187). Have students figure out approximately where Billie Jo lives and mark it on their maps. Then ask them to mark other places mentioned in the novel, such as the state of California and the cities of Lubbock, Amarillo, Dallas, Flagstaff, and Moline. What part does each place play in the novel? Which of these places are inside the Dust Bowl and which are outside?

Living with polio On President Franklin Delano Roosevelt's birthday, Billie Jo plays for a ball to collect money for infantile paralysis. Challenge students to research the connection between President Roosevelt and polio and find out why polio no longer poses the serious threat that it did in Billie Jo's time. Students can explore what they've learned in two or three journal entries in which they write from the perspective of a person who was stricken with polio. Be sure they mention the symptoms they might have

suffered and what their doctors have told them. Students can refer to the "Famous Polio People" page at **http://geocities.com/Heartland/Ranch/5212/poliopeople.html**. Follow the link to "People, Remembrances, and History" for survivor stories. A useful book is *Small Steps: The Year I Got Polio* by Peg Kehret (Albert Whitman, 1996).

Poetry Billie Jo comes to understand that the worst times are about losing spirit and hope. Invite students to write a poem about one of their worst experiences, using the free verse, nonrhyming poetry with which she tells her story as a model. *River Friendly, River Wild* by Jane Kurtz (Simon & Schuster, 2000) provides another model of free verse used in a first-person narrative to talk about surviving a disaster.

Faces of the Dust Bowl Study the cover photograph, taken in 1936 by Walker Evans. Dorothea Lange was another photographer who took many pictures of people in the Dust Bowl, helping the rest of the world understand what people were going through. Go to the Library of Congress site at **http://lcweb.loc.gov/ammen/fsahtml/fahome.html** to look at some of these pictures and the expressions on the people's faces. Let each student choose two different photos and write a detailed caption about what the person in the picture might have been thinking and experiencing. Print out the photos and display them with the captions beneath.

Dust Bowl hows and whys—weather Point out to students that many factors caused the Dust Bowl, including weather patterns, and have them list as many causes as they can find. Then have them list all the reasons they can think of to explain why the U.S. has never had another Dust Bowl of that magnitude. To help them complete their lists, direct them to resources recommended in Find Out More and consider inviting a meteorologist from the local network television station or the National Weather Service or a professor from a local college or university to speak about dust storms today.

Key Scenes by Season
Out of the Dust

Billie Jo divides her story into six seasons. For each of the seasons listed below, decide on the key scene and draw it in the middle of the box. In the border of the picture, use symbols and/or color or other ways to show what the weather is doing around Billie Jo.

Winter 1934	**Spring 1934**
Summer 1934	**Autumn 1934**
Winter 1935	**Spring 1935**

Justin and the Best Biscuits in the World

Mildred Pitts Walter

Knopf, 1986

Summary

Justin chafes at the instructions his mama and sisters give him and feels incompetent cleaning his room and doing other "women's work." So he's thrilled when his grandfather invites him to the ranch that has been in the family since the time of the great cattle drives; he's following in the footsteps of the great African-American cowboys. But Justin learns more than he bargained for: Grandpa teaches him not only to tighten cinches on horses but also to wash dishes and make biscuits—and about family history. As Grandpa says, "You must know where you've come from in order to find the way to where you want to go."

Background

Although Justin and his family live in Missouri, this book appears in the Southwest section because most of the activities relate to cowboy culture of the Southwest. This is a good opportunity to point out the way regions overlap. Do students know how many states had or still have working cowboys (as Grandpa describes himself), for instance? In fact, working cowboys have made their livings in most of the midwestern, southwestern, and western states.

After the Civil War, Texas was home to as many as 8,000 African-American cowboys—some who had been brought to Texas as slaves, others who had been escaped slaves hiding out in the big state, and still others who had come as soldiers with the Union army. The cook of the cowboy crews, who was often African American, Mexican, or German, had to work in the face of stampedes, blizzards, dust, storms, floods, and rattlesnakes. He was the total master of his own space, second in rank only to the boss. Cooks were sometimes called "pot rustlers" and sometimes "sourdoughs" because each cook nurtured his sourdough starter for months or even years, taking it to bed with him if necessary to keep it warm.

 Book Pairing

An excellent book for more information about the "night riders" in Justin's background is *Forty Acres and Maybe a Mule* by Harriette Gillem Robinet (Aladdin, 1998).

Note that the activities in this section are rich with book resources for grades 4 to 8 due to the unusual number of cowboy books available.

Find Out More

Cowboys in literature "A Reading and Language Arts Teacher Resources" page at **http://www.mhschool.com/teach/reading/mhreading/teachres/tes/4/4-2-2.html** offers many links to topics such as Bill Pickett, cowboy Africans in the diaspora, and more.

About the author The "Colorado Women's Hall of Fame" page at **http://www.cogreatwomen.org/walter.htm** has information about the author.

Hands-on Activities

Map it Grandpa talks about the history of cowboys. Familiarize students with the famous trails where cowboys drove cattle from Texas to the Midwest by having them trace these routes on a copy of a regional map in different colors. If students use the Internet, direct them to "Trail Drives of the Old West" at **http://www.net.westhost.com/trail1.htm**.

Illustrating a scene Invite students to draw or paint scenes from the many different places described in this novel. Half the class can work on scenes from four different settings: Justin's house (be sure to have students suggest likely places where he might live), the Q.T. Ranch, the fair, and Tennessee. Meanwhile, the other half can draw scenes from three journeys: the journey that Justin and Grandpa take to the ranch; the journeys that Great-Great-Grandfather Ward took as a cowboy from Texas to Kansas; and the journey that Great-Great-Grandfather Ward took from Tennessee to Missouri. You might display the scenes as a bulletin board to highlight both students' understanding of the setting of the book and their art work.

Rodeo diorama Encourage students to learn as much as they can about rodeos. A good resource is *Let's Rodeo!* by Robert Crum (Simon & Schuster, 1996). You can learn more about one of the famous African-American cowboys Grandpa talks about by reading the picture book *Bill Pickett: Rodeo-Ridin' Cowboy* by Andrea Pinkney (Harcourt, 1996). Each student or pair of students can choose a rodeo event and make a shoe box diorama with an accompanying description.

Outfit a cowboy Have students investigate the practical use for every article of cowboy clothing. One excellent resource, the picture book *Boss of the Plains* by Laurie Carlson (DK Ink, 1998), explains how John Stetson invented the famous Stetson or ten-gallon hat after he moved west to make his fortune in the gold rush—and what it's useful for. Two others, *The Cowboy ABC* by Chris Demarest (DK Ink, 1999) and *Cowboy Alphabet* by James Rice (Pelican, 1990), provide good information about other gear. To illustrate their knowledge, students can create a life-sized paper cutout of a cowboy that illustrates what they've learned about the use of each piece of clothing.

Writing like a cowboy Two picture books to give students fun ideas for their own cowboy writing are *Cowboy Dreams* by Kathi Appelt (HarperCollins, 1999) and *Bubba the Cowboy Prince* by Helen Ketteman (Scholastic, 1997). Invite students to capture cowboy culture in a cowboy lullaby, tall tale, or alphabet book.

Cowboy compositions Play a recording of the song "Rodeo" by Garth Brooks (*Ropin' the Wind*, Capitol, 1991) for students or teach them some of the old cowboy songs, such as "Home on the Range," which the cowboys would sing through the night to keep the cattle calm (and themselves awake). A cassette of *Black Texicans: Balladeers and Songsters of the Texas Frontier* can be ordered from the Rounder catalog at **http://www.rounder.com**. Encourage students to write their own cowboy song to one of the old tunes.

Best biscuits tasting Tap into students' appetites to spark their interest in doing research: Have them each find a recipe for biscuits, then compare and contrast the ingredients and steps. Now compare how they taste by letting student groups make some of these recipes in your classroom if you have cooking facilities. Otherwise you might arrange with the cafeteria staff to let you borrow equipment (and to do the final baking for you!) or have parent volunteers supervise the preparation and baking at home and let students bring in the results. You can even elect judges and have a contest, as in the novel. For a noncompetetive alternative, make it a biscuit tasting in which students write comments about the quality of each biscuit in terms of height, color, taste, texture, and moistness. (Note: If you or parent volunteers want to try cooking the way the cowboys did, experiment with outdoor cooking, using a Dutch oven pan and charcoal briquettes below and above the pan.)

Act it out, partner Help students learn more about some of the cowboys Grandpa describes by directing them to the following resources: *The Black Cowboys* by Gina De Angelis (Chelsea House, 1997), *Cowboys* by Robert Miller (Silver Burdett, 1991), *Will Rogers: Cherokee Entertainer* by Elisabeth Sonneborn (Chelsea House, 1993), *The Black Cowboys* by John Wukovits (Chelsea House, 1997), *Black Cowboy, Wild Horses: A True Story* by Julius Lester (Dial, 1998). When students have completed their research, divide them into groups and challenge them to write skits that will show an important scene from the life of each cowboy they learned about.

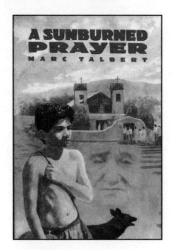

A Sunburned Prayer

Marc Talbert

Aladdin, 1995

Summary

Elroy's mother has to work and can't walk with Elroy on a pilgrimage to Chimayo on behalf of his abuelita, who is dying of cancer. She insists that an 11-year-old is too young to walk the 17 miles on his own. His father says, "Don't be stupid. If God answered our prayers we'd all be rich as Californians." His older brother gives him a mocking smile. But Elroy's grandmother is the only one who ever believed he was special, and Elroy will do anything to get the holy dirt to save her life.

Background

On Elroy's pilgrimage, he endures thirst, hunger, heat, and blisters. As he walks, he thinks about his ideas of God and experiences the small gifts of connecting with fellow travelers, especially a dog that makes the journey at his heels. Discuss what he hopes to find and what he actually does find. Note that Elroy occasionally uses coarse language, and you will want to talk about the meaning of the word *bitch*, its contemporary street use, and the complication of how it is used by Elroy in this novel.

For years, author Marc Talbert, who lives in Tesuque, New Mexico, watched people walking by his house on Good Friday. These were people on a pilgrimage to the Santuario de Chimayo in search of healing. He wondered would it be like to have such faith—and whether a person's faith would be shaken if the hoped for healing didn't come. Finally, he took his own pilgrimage, and that journey inspired him to write *A Sunburned Prayer*, a book that became a *School Library Journal* Best Book of the Year.

Book Pairing

This House Is Made of Mud/Esta Casa Esta Hecha de Lodo by Ken Buchanan (Northland, 1994) provides students with pictures and information about the construction of adobe houses such as the one Elroy lives in.

Find Out More

New Mexico Depending on where you live, your students may need a thorough introduction to the Spanish and Native American presence in New Mexico. These Web sites can help:

★ State of New Mexico at **http://www.rr.gmcs. k12.nm.us/dNMhist.htm** provides a history of New Mexico.

★ The Pueblo Indian Cultural Center site at **http://www.indianpueblo.org/ nambe. html** provides information on the Pueblo Indians, including Nambe Pueblo.

★ New Mexico Tribes at **http://www.kstrom.net/ isk/maps/nm/nmmap.html** provides links to information about New Mexico tribes and Rio Grande pueblos.

Hands-on Activities

Graphic organizer: A Tree Grows in . . . New Mexico (page 75) Have students use this Venn diagram to show which of the trees in Elroy's New Mexico are the same as the trees in your geographic region and which are unique to your region and to Elroy's. Extend their learning by having students create illustrated entries for each tree they investigate. Compile the entries into regional field guides.

Map it Work with the class to generate a list of all the place names in the novel, such as Chimayo, Chupadero, Rio en Medio, Santa Fe, Santa Fe National Forest, Jemez Mountains, Rio Grande, Nambe Lake, Tesuque, Cuyamungue, Camel Rock, Las Barrancas, Pojoaque, Espanola, and Pedernal. In order to understand the real-life setting of the novel, encourage students to study a map of New Mexico. Most of the places on Elroy's 17-mile journey will be easy to find, including the four-lane highway to Espanola that he walks along. If a place is not marked on the map (e.g., Camel Rock), help students recognize two possibilities: 1) that sometimes a novelist creates a fictional site and places it in a real land-scape, and 2) that some landmarks are too small to show up on most maps. Students can guess at what Elroy might mean when he talks about crossing "Indian land" (perhaps Santo Domingo or Tesuque or Nambe or Pojoaque Indian Reservation) or the mountains he looks at, "their black outlines now rimmed with frosty light" (page 12): perhaps the Sangre de Cristo range.

Badlands in the U.S. Talbert describes Las Barrancas as the "badlands of naked clay and sand [that] rose from the valley floor and had always looked like the backbones of dinosaurs to Elroy" (p. 50). Have students look up the word *badlands* and consider how this type of feature earned such a name. They can then study a topographical map and investigate which other states have "badlands" and, finally, create a map of the United States and Central America that shows the badlands.

A view of Chimayo Take students on a virtual trip to Roadsideamerica.com at **http://www.roadsideamerica.com/attract/ NMCHIshrine.html** to look at the shrine Elroy visits. Then have them use the visual details they've absorbed to write a journal entry from Elroy's point of view, remembering back to everything he saw once he reached the shrine at Chimayo that day.

Word meanings in context Marc Talbert sprinkles *A Sunburned Prayer* with Spanish words such as *abuela, perra,* and *mucha-cho.* As students begin to read, work with them to create their own glossaries for the Spanish words in the first chapter. Encourage them to figure out the definitions from the context of the story. Then, to help them gauge their accuracy, have them compare their definitions with the ones at the back of the book. Since Spanish-speaking students may already know these words, add (or have students add) to the class list challenging English words from the book.

Place name histories The name of Mark Twain's birthplace, Hannibal, sounds strange to Elroy and his brother, who confuse it with "cannibal." Students can work with maps of New Mexico to make a list of names of towns and cities in this state that come from the Spanish language, such as San Ignacio, Aqua Fria, and La Jara. Have them use a Spanish-English dictionary to figure out what the names mean and record these meanings on the list. Help students see history from a local perspective by inviting a speaker from the historical society to talk about the origins of place names where you live.

A Tree Grows in . . . New Mexico
A Sunburned Prayer

Use this Venn diagram to show which of the trees mentioned in *A Sunburned Prayer* are the same as the trees in your geographic region (overlap area) and which are unique to your region (left oval) and to Elroy's (right oval). Next to each tree name you list, illustrate the leaf or needle that is characteristic of that tree.

Trees Growing in Both Regions

Trees in Your
Geographic Region

Trees Growing Along the
Route Elroy Travels

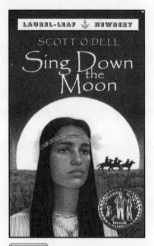

Sing Down the Moon

Scott O'Dell

Yearling, 1970

Recorded Books

Summary

Fourteen-year-old Bright Morning is kidnapped by Spanish slave traders and forced to work as a maid in a Mexican village. Her determination helps her escape, but in the process, Tall Boy, the young warrior she will later marry, is wounded, costing him the use of his arm. Worse is yet to come when the "Long Knives" destroy all the Navajo homes and fields in Canyon de Chelly. Bright Morning's clan joins other Navajo clans streaming out of their homelands toward resettlement, a journey that came to be known as the Long Walk. Will Bright Morning's stubborn vision be enough to guide her small family—Tall Boy, herself, and their young son—back to the canyon where she grew up?

Background

Scott O'Dell, renowned for his historical fiction, received a Newbery Honor Award for *Sing Down the Moon*, a story set in the mid 1860s when traditional Navajo life was coming to an end. His main character, Bright Morning, tells her terrifying and sad story in a calm, almost detached way in which silences speak volumes. Look at pages 21, 58, 73, and 90 for subtle clues that the story is, in fact, being told by an older person recalling her memories.

An author's note offers historical background. You may want to explain to students that the Penitentes, first mentioned on page 46, are a Catholic group of Spanish colonists. These Penitentes preserved Medieval rituals not generally practiced by most Catholics, including the very realistic reenactment of the crucifixion briefly woven into the plot of *Sing Down the Moon*.

 Book Pairing

Navajo: Voices and Visions Across the Mesa by Shonto Begay (Simon & Schuster, 1995) is a powerful look into Navajo culture through paintings and poems.

Find Out More

Canyon de Chelly Desert USA Magazine offers photos of Canyon de Chelly on its page "The Anasazi" at **http://www.desertusa.com/ind1/du_peo_ana.html**.

Literature guide "*Sing Down the Moon*: Student Background Resources" at the Curry School of Education site at **http://curry.edschool.virginia.edu/curry/dept/edlf/Heaton/owen/studentpage.html** provides book-related links to topics such as Kit Carson, Bosque Redondo, Fort Defiance, and a Navajo time line.

Hands-on Activities

Graphic organizer: Long Walk/Trail of Tears Comparison (page 78) Help students understand the history behind the events of *Sing Down the Moon* in a larger context of U.S./Native-American relations. Have them read about and then compare and contrast the Long Walk with the Trail of Tears. Students can fill in the graphic organizer to show when each relocation occurred, the number of people who walked, the starting and ending points of the routes they followed, the area in which each group resettled, and the people responsible for organizing and supervising the relocation.

Good resources for studying the Trail of Tears include *The Journal of Jesse Smoke: A Cherokee Boy, Trail of Tears*, 1838 by Joseph Bruchac (Scholastic, 2001) and *Only the Names Remain: The Cherokees and the Trail of Tears* by Alex Bealer (Little, Brown, 1972).

Map it Students may better appreciate the difficulty of Bright Morning's journey by tracing on a copy of a regional map the path she may have traveled to Mexico and back. Have students use a different color to show the path she and her people traveled from their home to Bosque Redondo. As students work on their maps, ask them if they can find any landmarks to add based on Bright Morning's memories of the journey.

Navajo ceremonies In Chapter 13, Bright Morning describes what it's like for her to go through *Kin-nadl-dah* or her Womanhood Ceremony. Read aloud or have students read on their own *Kinaaldá: A Navajo Girl Grows Up* by Monty Roessel (Lerner, 1993) to learn more about Navajo coming-of-age ceremonies today. How similar or different is Bright Morning's experience to that described in the nonfiction book?

Following the phases of the moon Send students on a search through the book to find all references to the moon, an important indicator of time passage. As they find references, have students make a list of all the ways Bright Morning makes use of the moon. With this information, students can research the phases of the moon and write an explanation for how much time has passed when Bright Morning says, "A new moon showed in the west and grew full and waned and still we moved on" (page 97). A book that shows people living by the patterns of the moon is *An Algonquian Year: The Year According to the Full Moon* by Michael McCurdy (Clarion, 2000).

Sheepherding comparison Invite students to connect literature and contrast different ways of life between two different U.S. agrarian cultures. Have them write an exchange of letters between Bright Morning and Ben, the main character in *The Loner* (see Mountain section, page 92), comparing what they know about sheep, how they feel about sheep, and how they care for their sheep.

Native American cultures presentation Although Bright Morning is Navajo, many other Native American groups are mentioned in the novel. Divide the class into groups to research the traditional lives (at this same time period) of the Ute (11), Nez Percé (30), Hopi (33), Zuni (34), Arapaho and Cheyenne (105), Apache (103), and Kiowa (33). Let the groups present their findings to the class in a creative way, such as a poster display, a documentary-style report, or a play.

Navajo life then and now Discuss how Navajo life today differs from Navajo life during the 1860s, as described by Scott O'Dell. Refer students to *Songs from the Loom: A Navajo Girl Learns to Weave* by Monty Roessel (Lerner, 1995) for information on modern-day Navajo life. To show what they've learned, students can create a set of drawings that illustrate some of the differences between Bright Morning's life at Canyon de Chelly and the life of a Navajo girl today.

Long Walk/Trail of Tears Comparison

Sing Down the Moon

Use the comparison matrix below to compare and contrast the Long Walk with another devastating event in U.S. history, the Trail of Tears. As you read about the migrations of Native American groups, forced to leave their lands and "relocated" by the government to distant places, take notes on the following to complete this page: when each relocation occurred, the number of people who walked, the starting and ending points of the routes they followed, the area in which each group resettled, and the people responsible for organizing and supervising the relocation.

	The Long Walk	The Trail of Tears
Date(s) when walk took place		
Number of people who walked		
Starting point of the "relocation"		
Ending point of the "relocation"		
Area of permanent resettlement		
Persons or groups responsible for organizing and supervising the "relocation"		

Search for the Shadowman

Joan Lowery Nixon

Yearling, 1996

Summary

As Andy, a boy from Hermosa, Texas, works on a class assignment to write about his family history, he discovers an ancestor who seems to have been deliberately obliterated. After discovering that the young man was believed to have stolen the family's money, causing great pain, Andy becomes determined to clear Coley Joe's name. But someone wants Andy to quit his digging—and it appears that the "someone" might be Andy's best friend. Andy won't stop, though. He uses the Internet, interviews, a graveyard, and library research to try to find the truth.

Background

Texas is the largest of the "lower 48" states, so big and diverse that at one time in U.S. history some legislators thought it should be carved into five separate states. Indeed, it has six distinct geographical regions (see page 81). *Search for the Shadowman* provides a good introduction to the varied geography and to 1800s Texas history, as Andy stumbles onto the mystery surrounding one of his ancestors, Coley Joe, born in 1856.

Joan Lowery Nixon is known for her fast-paced mysteries for young readers and is a multiple winner of the Edgar Allan Poe Award for best juvenile mystery. She says, "A mystery begins to develop in my mind when something sparks an idea and a question grows from it."

Book Pairing

Compare *Search for the Shadowman* with another mysterious book, *Holes*, the Newbery Award–winning novel by Louis Sachar (Farrar, Straus & Giroux, 1998). How does each author set up the mystery? What trail of clues leads to the solving of the mystery? At what point in each novel is the mystery solved? Can your students draw any conclusions about the genre of mystery novels from looking at these two books?

Find Out More

About the author Random House.com at **http://www.randomhouse.com/teachers/ authors/nixo.html** provides background information about Joan Lowery Nixon.

Author interview Book Page Online at **http://www.bookpage.com/9704bp/ childrens/joanlowerynixon.html** features an interview, "Jean [sic] Lowrey [sic] Nixon Weaves Mysteries from Past and Present."

Literature guide The *Search for the Shadowman* page at Random House.com at **http://www. randomhouse.com/teachers/guides/trc_inter. html#hist** provides good background information and links to topics related to the book.

Genealogy Andy is captivated by genealogy after he uncovers a skeleton in his own family closet. Two books that will help students trace their pasts and stories are *Do People Grow on Family Trees? Genealogy for Kids and Other Beginners* by Ira Wolfman (Workman, 1991) and *The Great Ancestor Hunt: The Fun of Finding Out Who You Are* by Lila Perl (Clarion, 1990). Students can also find information at "The Genealogy Home Page" at **http://www.genhomepage.com/**.

Hands-on Activities

Graphic organizer: Know Those Texas Regions (page 81) As *Search for the Shadowman* shows, Texas is a big state with regions that are quite different from each other. Encourage students to research these regions: East/Piney Woods, West Texas, the Panhandle, South Texas (including the Rio Grande Valley), Central Texas (including the Hill Country), and North Texas. Have them start their search with the information given in the novel and then look for other resources to help them complete the comparison. Let students use the chart to record the similarities and differences in weather and climate, topography, and features. Ask them to recall the following: In which region does Andy live? Where did Malcolm John Bonner and his family live before they moved? Where did Coley Joe's travels take him?

Map it Build a context for the setting of *Search for the Shadowman*: Have students create a Texas state map that includes the places mentioned in the novel, including rivers, mountains, and salt deposits. Then have them draw the route the settlers took from Corpus Christi to Hermosa and the route Coley Joe took to El Paso and San Elizario. Finally, students can try to locate and use symbols to mark an example of each Texas feature listed in the Author's Note.

Reporting a different story Andy makes a decision not to reveal what he has learned about Coley Joe, because although it would clear his ancestor's name, it would hurt his best friend's family. Spark students' creative thinking by having them imagine that Andy makes a different decision about telling what happened to Coley Joe and that they are the reporters who are assigned to write the story. Encourage students to write a list of people they would want to interview and the questions they would ask each person. When students have discussed their questions and possible answers, ask them to write a headline and the lead paragraph of this news story.

Outhouses and poke bonnets: A report on the past Andy takes notes as Miss Winnie and his grandparents talk about such things as country stores, oil lamps, dust storms, mosquitoes, high-buttoned shoes, poke bonnets, petticoats, outhouses, sock darning, electricity, cow milking, and fudge. Mr. Hammergren gives Andy an A on his family's oral history report (page 148), but the reader doesn't get to read it. Have your class set out to write "Andy's Family: An Oral History Report About the Way People Used to Live." Assign a student or group of students to each topic and ask them to do research, using books or interviews with senior citizens in the community. Each student or group should then write the piece of Andy's report that he or she has researched.

Character letter exchange Divide students into letter-writing pairs, with one student taking the role of Andy and the other taking the role of Coley Joe Bonner. The student who is writing for Andy should start with the question, "Why would anyone want to fight a war over salt?" Require that the pairs write at least one exchange of letters, each letter explaining about salt in that character's time: where they get it, what it's used for, how much it costs, and how people feel about it. Students will need to do some research, especially to write from Coley Joe's point of view.

Know Those Texas Regions

Search for the Shadowman

As *Search for the Shadowman* shows, Texas is a big state with regions that are quite different from each other. Starting with the information you find in the book, gather information about these regions: East/Piney Woods, West Texas, the Panhandle, South Texas (including the Rio Grande Valley), Central Texas (including the Hill Country), and North Texas. Fill in the chart below to show similarities and differences in weather and climate, topography, and features.

Region	Weather and Climate	Topography	Well-known Natural Features or Cities
East/Piney Woods			
West Texas			
Panhandle			
South Texas			
Central Texas			
North Texas			

Notice the way these regions play a role in *Search for the Shadowman*:

★ In which region does Andy live? _____

★ Where did Malcolm John Bonner and his family live before they moved? _____

★ Where did Coley Joe's travels take him? _____

Mountain

Featured Regional Readings

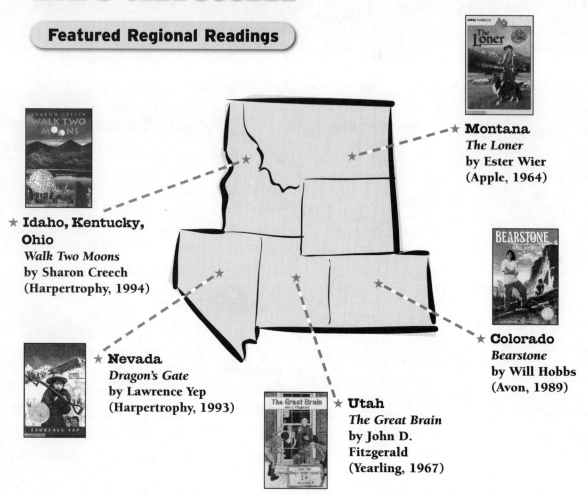

★ **Montana**
The Loner
by Ester Wier
(Apple, 1964)

★ **Idaho, Kentucky, Ohio**
Walk Two Moons
by Sharon Creech
(Harpertrophy, 1994)

★ **Colorado**
Bearstone
by Will Hobbs
(Avon, 1989)

★ **Nevada**
Dragon's Gate
by Lawrence Yep
(Harpertrophy, 1993)

★ **Utah**
The Great Brain
by John D. Fitzgerald
(Yearling, 1967)

Other Recommended Regional Readings

★ **Montana**

Rescue Josh McGuire by Ben Mikaelsen (Hyperion, 1991)

Wolf at the Door by Barbara Corcoran (Atheneum, 1993)

★ **Utah**

All Is Well by Kristin Embry Litchman (Yearling, 1998)

The Blue Between the Clouds by Stephen Wunderli (Holt, 1996)

★ **Wyoming**

Dangerous Ground by Gloria Skurzynski (Bradbury, 1989)

Jenny of the Tetons by Kristiana Gregory (Harcourt, 1989)

Red Dog by Bill Wallace (Pocket, 1987)

★ **Yellowstone Park**

The Absolutely True Story of How I Visited Yellowstone With the Terrible Rupes by Willo Davis Roberts (Atheneum, 1994)

Bearstone

Will Hobbs

Avon, 1989

 Recorded Books

If your students enjoy *Bearstone*, introduce them to the sequel, *Beardance*, in which Cloyd attempts to make amends for his part in the death of a grizzly bear (in *Bearstone*) by helping two bear cubs survive through a Colorado winter.

Summary

Cloyd has been raised by his grandmother with plenty of time to wander until he's sent off to the Ute group home. Walter, an old widower, agrees to let the troubled 14-year-old work on his farm for the summer. After running away, where he discovers a turquoise bear hidden in an ancient burial site, Cloyd discovers he actually likes working for Walter. But the teenager, who has given himself the secret name of Lone Bear, erupts and destroys everything he's built when he meets Walter's bear hunter friends. High in the mountains at Walter's gold mine, will Cloyd be able to reconnect with the old man?

Background

As *Bearstone* opens, Cloyd is scheming to get himself inside a hospital room, having hitch-hiked to Arizona to find the father he never knew. He succeeds, only to find that his father is brain-dead, a "shrunken shell of a human being." Talk with students about why the author chose to begin this way. Note that by the end of the novel, Walter has become a new father figure for Cloyd.

Find Out More

About the author You can read Will Hobbs's biography, find out where he got the idea for *Bearstone*, and read about *Beardance* on the author's Web site at **http://www. willhobbsauthor.com** by clicking on each cover.

The Ute These Web sites provide information on the culture and history that play a part in Cloyd's family background:

★ Blue Mountain Arts "Ute Indians" page at **http://bvsd.k12.co.us/schools/mont/topics/ UteIndians/UteIndians.html**

★ Strings in the Mountains "The Ute Indians" page at **http://www.stringsinthemountains. org/m2m/ute.htm** (student-written page)

Navajo Find another school-created site with information about the Navajo at the Study of Native Americans "The Navaho" page at **http://inkido.indiana.edu/w310work/romac/ navajo.htm**.

Bears Learn how to tell the difference between a black bear and a grizzly and other bear facts at "The Bear Den" at Nature Net: **http://www. nature-net.com/bears/brown.html**.

Hands-on Activities

Graphic organizer: Charting Cloyd's Skills (page 85) Lead a discussion about Cloyd's resourcefulness. Ask students if they can identify the new skills and knowledge he gains over the course of the novel. Have students fill in this chart with their list of Cloyd's skills and then identify who taught him each skill and when he learned it. In the last column, students can try to imagine how Cloyd might use the skill in the future he has chosen for himself. (Skills students might list include using a chain saw, housekeeping, bear tracking, gold mining, reading, and writing.)

Map it Encourage students to explore the setting for this book and the geography of the Mountain region. Have students make a list of places mentioned in the novel, including Salt Lake City, White Mesa, Monument Valley, Window Rock, Missouri, Texas, Durango, Blanding, New Mexico, Monarch Pass, Silverton, Pine River, Snowslide Creek, and so on. Students should label each place on the list a state, a city or town, or a geographic feature. Now have them look at a U.S. map and a Colorado state map to locate all the places they've listed. At **http://www.topozone.com**, students can type into the map finder a name such as Ute Lake or Rio Grande Pyramid.

Character conversations Cloyd's grandmother tells him their band of Weminuche Utes haven't always lived at White Mesa, Utah; the mountains above Durango, Colorado, were their home until gold was discovered there. Get students involved in exploring the regional and historical issues that characters from different regional books have in common. Give them the following assignment choices: (1) Write a conversation that Lucy Whipple, the main character in *The Ballad of Lucy Whipple* (Pacific section, page 101), and Cloyd might have comparing their thoughts about gold fever. (2) Write a conversation that Otter, the main character in *Dragon's Gate* (Mountain section, page 86), and

Cloyd might have about mining. (3) Write a conversation David, the main character in *The Loner* (Mountain section, page 92), and Cloyd might have about grizzly bears. The conversation can be set as a narrative dialogue or in a simple script format, depending on students' level of sophistication.

An archaeologist's journal entry Cloyd in *Bearstone* and Bright Morning in *Sing Down the Moon* (Southwest section, page 76) both find caves that were used by the Ancient Ones. Review these passages with students and invite them to imagine that they are archaeologists studying one of those caves today. They should write a page from their journal describing what they have discovered. Students can find information on cave art in *Native American Rock Art: Messages from the Past* by Yvette La Pierre (Lickle Publishing, 1994), with its description of how archaeologists interpret what people leave behind, and *The Ancient Cliff Dwellers of Mesa Verde* by Caroline Arnold (Clarion, 1992), with its pictures of archaeologists at work. A helpful Web site with photos of Canyon de Chelly, one place where ancient ruins have been found, is *Desert USA Magazine* at **http://www.desertusa.com/ind1/du_peo_ana.html**.

A taste of Ute culture: fry bread Cloyd talks fondly about his grandmother's fry bread, a staple of many powwows and other festive events. If you want to try making it with the class, you can find recipes on the Web along with descriptions of powwows. Check out "Best Indian Fry Bread Ever" at **http://www.casagrande.com/oodham/frybread.html** and "Secrets to Perfect Fry Bread" at **http://www.redcorn.com/html/secrets.html**.

Persuasive paragraphs One of the questions Cloyd thinks about is, Do horses care? Using the novel (and possibly books about horses) to gather evidence, students can write persuasive paragraphs that support their responses to Cloyd's question.

Charting Cloyd's Skills
Bearstone

Cloyd is a resourceful character who gathers new skills and knowledge over the course of the novel. Use the chart below to make a list of his skills and identify who taught him each skill and when he learned it. In the last column, try to imagine how Cloyd might use the skill in the future he has chosen for himself.

Skill	When?	Who?	Future?
Riding horseback	Childhood	Grandmother	Ride with Walter to explore the mountains more thoroughly

 Recorded Books

Dragon's Gate
Laurence Yep
HarperTrophy, 1993

Summary

Otter, a privileged and somewhat sheltered boy in Hwangtung Province, China, idolizes his father and Uncle Foxfire who work in faraway America, the Land of the Golden Mountain. After Otter accidentally kills a Manchu soldier, he has to flee to San Francisco. To his dismay, when he finds his father and uncle, they are not leaders and lords but laborers in the snow tunnels of the mountain they call the Tiger, and Otter is now in a place of great danger from railroad work, the natural elements, and the crew bosses.

Background

In *Children's Books and Their Creators* edited by Anita Silvey (Houghton Mifflin, 1995), Laurence Yep notes that anyone who writes historical fiction for children can draw on facts, dates, and statistics—but that if he had encountered only dry, second-hand sources, he probably would never have written his historical fiction books. Instead, much of his work was fueled by his father's stories about his memories of China. Yep has won several Newbery Honor awards for his historical fiction, including one for *Dragon's Gate*.

Before the Civil War, the North and South disagreed about the best route for a railway across the country. During the war, Congress appropriated funds for the railroad, and construction

began in 1863. Workers who started from the eastern end (in the Midwest) included many Irish immigrants. Those who started on the West Coast were mostly Chinese immigrants. They met six years later, in 1869, at Promontory Point, Utah. The president of the Central Pacific Railroad lifted the hammer to drive in a last spike made of gold. He took a mighty swing—and missed, making the railroad workers hoot with laughter.

 Book Pairing

Not everyone was thrilled with the new railroad that crossed the United States. Read *Death of the Iron Horse* by Paul Goble (Aladdin, 1987) to expose students to the toll railroad construction took on natural habitats and Native American cultures.

Find Out More

About the author Laurence Yep has said in interviews that when he was growing up, he found nothing to read about the lives of Chinese Americans. Pictures and an interview are in *Author Talk* edited by Leonard S. Marcus (Simon & Schuster, 2000) or on the Web by following links at Internet School Library Media Center at **http://falcon.jmu.edu/~ramseyil/yep.htm**.

Promontory Point You can see a picture of the driving in of the last spike and many others at "New Perspectives on The West" at **http://www. pbs.org/weta/thewest/** (Episode 5) or in a companion book, *The West: An Illustrated History*

for Children by Dayton Duncan (Little Brown, 1996).

Chinese-American culture and history Other excellent links are at **http://eduscapes.com/ newbery/94c.html**, in which educators and authors Annette Lamb and Nancy Smith explore such subjects as Chinese immigrants, the transcontinental railroad, and labor and immigration laws; and at McGraw-Hill's "Reading & Language Arts" site at **http://www.mhschool. com/student/reading/mhreading/6/6-1-3.html**, which features a Chinese-American time line.

Hands-on Activities

Graphic organizer: Character Comparison: Sean and Otter (page 88) Sean and Otter show great interest in each other's cultures. Encourage students to fill in this comparison matrix to highlight some of the similarities and differences they discover. Students will need to find evidence from *Dragon's Gate* to compare the characters in these categories: food, language, opportunity for and feelings about education, jobs in the tunnel, memories of childhood, clothing, attitudes of relatives toward people of other cultures, and reason for wandering the tunnels.

Map it Have students make a map that hightlights in different colors each railroad built before 1900. They can use a U.S. outline map and colored pencils along with an encyclopedia, history book, or the Internet at "Transcontinental Railroad Lines" at **http://www. wwnorton.com/college/history/tindall/time linf/tranrail.htm** to find information on nineteenth-century railroad building in the U.S.

Old railroad maps Sean talks about how much he likes geography (pages 128–130). Students can see what kinds of maps Sean might have studied at the <u>Central Pacific Railraod Photographic History Museum</u> site at **http:// www.cprr.com/Museum/Maps/index.html**.

Have students scroll through the historical maps and list the differences between those maps and a modern map.

Otter and Yang: two Chinese-American stories Yang the Youngest and His Terrible Ear (see Pacific section, page 104) is a story of a modern-day Chinese boy who has emigrated to the United Sates. Invite students to make a list of some of the similarities and differences between Otter's and Yang's experiences. For example, Otter explains family name traditions on page 132 of *Dragon's Gate*. Compare this description with Yang's description on page 22 of *Yang the Youngest and His Terrible Ear*. Remind students to include the boys' experiences both in China and the U.S.

To help students understand more about China in Otter's lifetime, have them visit "Daily Life in Ancient China" at **http://members.aol.com/ Donnclass/Chinalife.html**. Another Web page that can help them understand Otter's life before he leaves his home is <u>China Vista</u> at **http://www. chinavista.com/**. Links that can help students imagine the strike sign Otter writes in Chinese (*Dragon's Gate*, page 249) so that Kilroy can't understand it include "Reading Chinese" at **http://pasture.ecn.purdue.edu/~agenhtml/ agenmc/china/chinese.html** and "Chinese Calligraphy: Language As Art" at <u>Think Quest</u> at **http://tqjunior.thinkquest.org/3614/**.

Research and writing Bright Star says, "The westerners' history books will write about what a big hero Kilroy was" (page 248). Ask students if Bright Star was right. Assign them to look up "railroads" in *World Book Encyclopedia* to discuss how the contributions of the railroad builders, including the Chinese workers, are described. Then have students write their own section for the encyclopedia, using some of what they learned in reading *Dragon's Gate*.

Character Comparison: Sean and Otter

Dragon's Gate

Sean and Otter show great interest in each other's cultures. Use the comparison matrix below to highlight some of the similarities and differences they discover.

	Sean	Otter
Food		
Language		
Opportunity for and feelings about education		
Job(s) in the tunnels		
Memories of childhood		
Clothing		
Attitudes of their relatives toward people of other cultures		
Reason for wandering the tunnels		

 Listening Library (Cliffhangers first chapter recording)

The Great Brain
John D. Fitzgerald
Yearling, 1967

Summary

J.D. is in awe of his middle brother, Tom, a.k.a. The Great Brain. Somehow for each of life's problems, Tom is able not only to find a solution but also to profit financially. Some of his schemes backfire. For instance, Mamma makes Tom give back all the pennies he collects from the town's youngsters who want to see the first water closet in a town full of outhouses. But many other schemes work. Will Tom demand the agreed-on payment for figuring out how a friend with an amputated leg can still do his chores and play, even with a wooden prosthetic leg?

Background

The author drew on his own boyhood memories in the late 1800s Utah to write this book, and the flavor is quite different from historical novels written about the same period (such as *The Ballad of Lucy Whipple*—see Pacific section, page 101). Before students start reading, they'll probably need to explore some of Fitzgerald's words and idioms (see the list in Vocabulary to know: Utah-isms).

Although Papa and Momma are respectful and tolerant of everyone in the town—the Mormons, the Jewish peddler, the Greek immigrant family, and others—some of the prejudices common at the time come through: The boys of the town play "wild Indian" games, use the word *squaw*, and take an oath on the skull of a dead Indian chief that Tom's Uncle Mark gave him. This is a good opportunity to discuss a hot issue in current events: how Native American bones and remains have historically been treated.

Book Pairing

Read with students sections of *Give Me My Father's Body: The Life of Minik, the New York Eskimo* by Harper Kenn (Steerforth, 2000), a reprint of a 1986 book about the issue of the treatment of Native American ancestral remains.

Find Out More

Ute and Paiute history Direct students to these sites:

★ Utah Kids site at **http://www.dced.state.ut. us/history/ForKids/forkids.html**, which has a link for American Indians.

★ "The Ute Indians" at **http://www.stringsin themountains.org/m2m/ute.htm**.

★ Council on Indian Nations site at **http://www.cinprograms.org/people/ northern/paiute.html** offers a map of present-day Paiute reservations.

Hands-on Activities

✂️ *Activity page—Old-Fashioned Ice Cream Making (page 91)* Making ice cream was a common activity for families for many decades (see Fitzgerald's description on page 71 of *The Great Brain*). Encourage students to interview older family members, such as grandparents, to see if they have memories of the things J.D. describes. Then try this ice cream recipe in class or send it home with students to enjoy on their own.

🌐 **Map it** J.D. and his brothers live in a mostly Mormon community. Challenge students to make a map of the Mormon trail on which the ancestors of many of the town's founding citizens would have come west. If you want to use the Internet, visit Trail of Hope: The Story of the Mormon Trail at **http://www.pbs.org/trailofhope/**.

✏️ *Vocabulary to know: Utah-isms* Because this book was written in the 1960s by a man who was remembering his own childhood in the late 1800s, there are some words and terms you may want to have students learn before they begin to read (you might divide up the words among groups of students for short vocabulary presentations):

backhouse	kindling
barker	lariat
boarding house	litter
bonanza	loco
cesspool	pint flask
emporium	quarantined
flying mare	Sears Roebuck
gangrene	Sen Sen
gross receipts	strongbox
haymaker	tom-tom
icehouse	water closet
inkwell	wrist lock

📖 *"Games our grandparents played" booklet* Many games of the time period are mentioned in *The Great Brain*, including "Heavy, Heavy Hangs Over My Poor Head," "Button, Button, Who's Got the Button," kick the can, marbles, can stilts, fighting/wrestling, dominoes, erector set, one-o-cat, and jackass leapfrog. Once again, older adults make terrific primary sources. Have students interview senior citizens in the community to see how many of these games they can find out how to play. (Students can find more information at "Old Fashioned Children's Games" at **http://members.fortune city.com/sharonobryan/**.) When each student has documented a game and listed the rules, celebrate with a game day where students teach each other how to play the games they've researched. Once they've tried the game out, they may find that they need to go back to their interview source to clarify some rules or other points. Encourage them to write out the revised instructions and helpful tips for playing each game and put the game descriptions together in a class booklet.

✂️ *Design for an outhouse* J.D.'s family is the first one in town to have an indoor toilet rather than an outhouse. At one time, outhouses were very common in the United States, and they still are used in some places today. Students can find out what they look like at "The Outhouse Gallery of Don Ponder" at **http://dponder.home. mindspring.com** and then design their own outhouses.

📊 *Paiute and Ute comparison chart* It's clear from the boys' talk and games that Native Americans are a part of their world. Papa invites Chief Tav-Wad-im from the Paiute to dinner, for instance. Two major Native American cultures existed in the area in which the book is set: the Southern Paiute and the Ute. (Do students recognize any similarities between the Ute name and the state's name? Point out that the state of Utah got its name from the Ute Indians.) Have students research the difference between these cultures. Students can use a T chart to list the similarities between the Utes and the Southern Paiutes. (They might compare where these groups lived, their food, housing, celebrations, and where they live today.)

Making Old-Fashioned Ice Cream
The Great Brain

J.D. describes making ice cream—the old-fashioned way—on page 71. Making ice cream was a common activity for families for many decades. Interview your own grandparents to see if they have memories of making ice cream with a hand-crank freezer bucket.

Now try this recipe: Kids ages 2 to 102 can make this ice cream with little muss or fuss—and it's delicious! You don't need an ice cream machine, and you don't need a freezer for hardening or storage, so you can make this recipe just about anywhere!

You will need
1/2 cup heavy whipping cream
1 tablespoon sugar
1/4 teaspoon vanilla extract
2 cups ice cubes (about two large handsfull)
6 tablespoons rock salt
1 sandwich-size sealable plastic bag
1 quart-size, or other large, sealable plastic freezer bag
1 pair of oven mitts
1 dish towel
1 spoon

What to do
1. Pour the cream into the sandwich-sized bag.
2. Add sugar and vanilla extract to the same bag.
3. Seal the bag. (Make sure it's tightly closed, otherwise your ingredients will leak.)
4. Place the closed sandwich bag inside the freezer bag.
5. Pour the ice into the freezer bag.
6. Pour the rock salt into the freezer bag.
7. Seal the freezer bag. Tightly, please!
8. Put on your oven mitts, or wrap the dishtowel loosely around the freezer bag.
9. Shake, rock, roll, and squeeze the bag for a full 5 minutes. (Note: The bag is going to get very cold, 18–20° F. The mitts or dish towel will keep your hands from freezing.)
10. Open the freezer bag and remove the sandwich bag. Using the dish towel, quickly wipe away any rock salt and water from the outside of the sandwich bag. (The ice will have almost completely melted, so the outside of your sandwich bag will be wet.) This will keep the salt and water out of your sandwich bag—and your ice cream!—when you open it.
11. Open the sandwich bag and . . . enjoy! You can eat the ice cream right out of the bag, or spoon it into a bowl.

—Adapted and used with permission from
We All Scream for Ice Cream! The Scoop on America's Favorite Dessert
by Lee Wardlaw (HarperCollins, 2000).

The Loner
Ester Wier
Apple, 1964

Summary

"The boy" can't remember having a mother or father. He's worked in the fields as long as he can remember, traveling with anyone who will give him shelter in exchange for his earnings. Once, he becomes close enough to a migrant girl that she almost gives him a name, but she's killed when her long yellow hair is caught in a potato-digging machine. Then he strikes out completely on his own and is taken in by Boss, a woman herding sheep in the mountains of Montana.

Background

When is this story set? Challenge students to try to figure it out. Very few clues are given. For instance, "the boy," later called David, is probably under fourteen. Other clues might be the trucks, old foot lockers, oil stoves, washtubs, carton boxes, mention of the "children's home," the goal of getting to California, the old Quonset hut in Texas, an abandoned railroad boxcar in Utah, and a shack in a growers' camp in Idaho. You can look at *Kids at Work: Lewis Hine and the Crusade Against Child Labor* by Russell Freedman (Clarion, 1998) to help figure out whether the story is set before or after child labor laws were passed by Congress.

Notice that Boss calls the bear that David ultimately kills a "devil wrapped in fur" and a "miserable, ornery, thieving killer" (page 83).

Discuss with your students the way attitudes toward bears have changed (and why) between the time Wier wrote this novel and the time that Hobbs wrote *Bearstone* (Mountain section, page 83).

 Book Pairing

What can students lean about the lives of migrant workers in the United States today? One good resource is *Migrant Worker: A Boy from the Rio Grande Valley* by Diane Hoyt-Goldsmith (Holiday House, 1996). They can use a T chart to compare and contrast migrant life in David's time and today.

Find Out More

Bear facts A good Web site with general information about bears is "The Bear Den" at **http://www.nature-net.com/bears/**.

Grizzly bears See if your library media specialist can locate an out-of-print book, *Hugh Glass, Mountain Man* by Robert McClung (Morrow, 1990) to learn about what happened when humans tangled with grizzlies back in the days when many of the bears roamed the mountains. Students can read about Lewis and Clark's own encounters with bears in *How We Crossed the West: The Adventures of Lewis and Clark* by Rosalyn Schanzer (National Geographic, 1997), or at "Discovering Lewis and Clark" at **http://www.lewis-clark.org**, where you can type "grizzly" in the search engine.

Montana To see pictures of the Montana mountains where David finds himself, go to <u>Northwest Montana</u> at **http://www.northwestmontana. com/** (students can look at live elk via webcam). They can also send a Montana postcard to a friend at <u>Travel Montana</u> at **http://travel.state. mt.us/postcards/**.

Hands-on Activities

Graphic organizer: Migrant Fields vs. Montana Comparison (page 94) What was David's life like before and after he got to Montana? Have students use the chart below to make the comparisons in the following areas of his life: people he spends time with, work/jobs he finds, the landscape, hardships and challenges he faces, survival skills he uses, and dreams for his future.

Map it Grizzly bears have a more widespread habitat than any of the other eight bear species. Have students use an encyclopedia and a world map to locate all the places they can be found in North America, Europe, and Asia.

Life-size grizzly Direct students to more information about grizzly bears at "The Cub Den" **http://www.nature-net.com/bears/cubden. html**. There they will learn such facts as these:

★ Adult bears are about 3 1/2 feet tall when on all fours. When they stand on their hind legs, they stretch from 6 1/2 to 7 feet tall.

★ They usually weigh anywhere from 330 to 825 pounds.

★ For short bursts, they can run 35 miles per hour.

★ Often, bears have front claws that are almost 5 inches long.

Provide students with long sheets of craft paper, markers, scissors, and tape. Using the above statistics and any other helpful information they can find, invite students to make a paper grizzly (standing or on all fours!) to display on the wall.

Guess who's talking about bears? Get students to generate a class list of some of the types of people who have come into contact with U.S. grizzly bears over the years—for example, mountain man (trapper), conservationist, Ute, rancher, hunter, farmer, photographer, settler, explorer (such as Lewis and Clark), hiker, camper, tourist, game warden. You can also include the names of characters from *The Loner*, such as Ben, David, and Boss. If the class has read *Bearstone* (Mountain section, page 83) and *Moose Tracks* (Midwest section, page 58), include appropriate character names from those books as well. Have each student or student group research the role of one of the people or characters on the list to find out how he or she interacts with bears. Then, pass out index cards. On the card, have students write two or three sentences about bears from the point of view of the person or character they researched. Put the cards in a bowl or hat. Have a student draw the cards and read the statements out loud. See if the rest of the class can guess who is speaking.

My new sheepdog Students can learn more about sheepherding by checking out "A Hearding Pup Takes Its First Steps" at **http://www. geocities.com/Heartland/Ranch/5093/pup development.html**. They'll read about a pup's first experiences with sheep and learning the basics of herding. Invite students to use what they've learned in two to three imaginative journal entries in which they describe what it's like to break in their new sheepdog.

Mountain poems Have students write a free-verse poem describing the mountains from David's point of view. Remind students to use the five senses and make comparisons ("When I fell down to sleep, the grass under my cheek felt like . . ."). Then write a poem about the Montana mountains from Sal's point of view (look at Chapter 35 in *Walk Two Moons*, see Mountain section, page 95) or Otter's point of view in *Dragon's Gate* (Mountain section, page 86). Discuss with students how the poems are similar and different.

Migrant Fields vs. Montana
The Loner

What was David's life like before and after he got to Montana? Use the the chart below to make the comparisons in each area of his life.

	Migrant Fields	Montana
People he spends time with		
Work/jobs		
Landscape		
Hardships and challenges		
Survival skills		
Dreams for his future		

Walk Two Moons
Sharon Creech

HarperTrophy, 1994

 Listening Library

Summary

Salamanca Tree Hiddle embarks on a long drive with Gramps and Gram—all the way from Euclid, Ohio, to Lewiston, Idaho—to try to bring her momma back home. To pass the time, Sal begins to relate a long story "about Phoebe Winterbottom, her disappearing mother, and the lunatic." As the three travel across country, the story becomes increasingly mysterious as the reader learns more about Sal's friend Phoebe, Sal's home in Kentucky and her new, temporary home in Ohio, her family, her friends, and her longing for her mother.

Background

For much of her adult life, Sharon Creech has divided her time between life in the U.S. and Great Britain, where she teaches American and British literature in a school where her husband is the headmaster. In an interview with British children's author Michael Thorne (found at "Achuka Interview" at **http://www.achuka.co. uk/scsg.htm**), she says that while she was writing *Walk Two Moons*, "I felt as if I was listening to Salamanca, letting her tell me her story. As the listener, I kept trying to pick up clues as to what was really on her mind." She adds, "I didn't have the vaguest idea what her story was when I began. I just liked her voice, and I followed her along. Each day, when I'd re-read the story from the beginning, I'd pick up a new 'clue,' and then I'd follow that thread."

This Newbery Award–winning novel has a complicated structure, but all the pieces of the various stories ultimately fit together. In the end, the reader understands what has really happened with Momma and why Sal needed this trip to learn to "walk two moons in another person's moccasins." Either while you read or after you finish the novel, go back and trace all the things Sal says about her mother in order to figure out the ways the author deliberately misleads the readers to create a surprise ending, without having Sal say or think anything untruthful.

 Book Pairing

For another lively and outrageous grand-mother in recent literature, encourage students to read *A Long Way from Chicago* (Dial, 1998) and *A Year Down Yonder* (Dial, 2000), two related books by Richard Peck. Since both books are made up of interrelated short stories, you can read one or two aloud to illustrate the flavor of the books.

Find Out More

Literature link You can find a review, discussion starters, activities, related Web sites, and a long list of suggestions on "Native Americans and Children's Literature" at Carol Hurst's Children's Literature site at **http://www.carolhurst.com/ newsletters/54anewsletters.html**.

Literature guides

★ A "Teacher CyberGuide" unit for *Walk Two Moons* from the Schools of California Online Resources for Educators (SCORE) at **http://www.sdcoe.k12.ca.us/score/walk/walktg.htm** is very thorough, with reflective questions and connections to language arts content standards as well as links to many related subjects, such as a Grandparents' Day contest, Mt. Rushmore history, Native American leaders, Longfellow's quotes, Yellowstone Day Hikes, and Dangerous and Venomous Organisms.

★ Find additional resources in "Sharon Creech's Walk Two Moons" at HarperCollins Teaching Guides at **http://www.harperchildrens.com/hch/parents/teachingguides/**.

Hands-on Activities

Map it Sal takes one journey from her home to Ohio and another with her grandparents to Idaho. Have students make a map that shows both journeys. Before they map out the journey to Idaho, help them get acquainted with the geography of the places mentioned in the book. See if students can locate on regional and state maps where Gramps might cross the Montana border into Idaho, the "curvy road" that Sal takes from Coeur d'Alene to Lewiston, Lewiston Hill, the Snake River, Pullman, and Longwood. On their own maps, students can include pictures of what Sal saw along the way.

Web of character relationships At first, it doesn't appear that there is any relationship among many of the people in Sal's long, rambling story, but in the end it becomes clear that almost everyone is connected to everyone else in some way. Work with students to create a web, with Sal at the middle, showing how the characters in the novel are related and interconnected.

What happened first? The plot of *Walk Two Moons* weaves and layers pieces of three different stories, including the narrative of Sal's trip, Sal's story of Phoebe Winterbottom, and Sal's mother's story. Help students place the chronological events of the novel in order, starting with the earliest thing they know about Sal's family in Kentucky and finishing at Bybanks, Kentucky.

Letters from scenic Idaho Ask students to imagine that Sal's mother was able to travel around Idaho and write a letter to Sal about all of the wonderful things she saw. Encourage students to do some research about scenic and interesting spots and pick some they think Chanhassen "Sugar" Hiddle might have liked because of the kind of person she was. Using this information, they can write a letter from Sugar to Sal describing those places. You can order an Idaho state map and travel guide from **http://www.visitid.org** or by calling 1-800-VISIT-ID.

Remembering Idaho After she goes back home, Sal will carry images of Idaho in her mind and heart. Invite students to imagine that Sal has grown up and had a daughter of her own. She thinks back to the journals that Mr. Birkway had the class keep and decides to keep a journal for her daughter. For her first entries, she writes and draws her memories of those days in Idaho. Have students create those pages.

Longing for Kentucky This time, invite students to imagine that Sal did decide to send postcards to her father, Phoebe, and Ben. Have students design a postcard from each of the stops all along the trip and write the message that would go on the back of each one. How might Sal write differently to each recipient? Consider having each student pick a destination and an audience. Create a bulletin board or other display with the postcards. Students might also create a scrapbook with pictures of all the things Sal misses about Kentucky.

Yellowstone geography Which states can say that Yellowstone belongs to them? Have students draw a map of Yellowstone National Park, which Sal visits with her grandparents, and mark in state boundaries. For Internet reference, direct students to The Official Web site of Yellowstone National Park at **http://www.nps. gov/yell/home.htm**, to plan what they would see and do if they took a trip to Yellowstone.

Yellowstone history See what students can find out about the earliest people to see the wonders of what became Yellowstone National Park, including the Shoshone people and mountain man John Colter. Ask: Who decided it should become a park, and when? What was the process for creating this oldest national park? With their answers to these questions, students can create a display that shows some of the wonders of Yellowstone National Park. Around the edges, they can illustrate different historical figures and characters (including Sal, her momma, and her grandparents) who gazed at those wonders.

Walk Two Moons glossary *Walk Two Moons* is full of interesting words—some that students won't find in the dictionary! Encourage students to notice how the following words are used in the story. Then, using definitions from the dictionary or from what they've gleaned from the context of the passage, students can write a glossary for *Walk Two Moons*, including these words and any others they think should be defined. Challenge students to apply their knowledge of the word meanings by including with the definition an example sentence that uses the word.

caboodle (1)
ding-dong (4)
tottery (5)
peculiarity (6)
squirt (11)
whang-doodle (12)
omnipotent (12)

defiance (15)
cadaver (22)
pepped-up (25)
damsel (27)
diabolic (29)
muesli (30)
thumpingly (32)

respectable (32)
huzza (37)
lunatic (41)
pandemonium (46)
shrapnel (54)
gullible (54)
piddly (55)
chickabiddy (59)
intriguing (60)
beef-brained (62)
flinch (65)
agenda (70)
slurping (78)
cowlike (80)
deprived (82)
pitiful (85)
ornery (90)
blazes (91)
bowie (93)
piddles (97)
warble (99)
crochety (102)
gooseberry (114)
cavorted (116)
smoothbeautifully (123)
malinger (132)
frenzy (132)
amnesia (137)
treacherous (143)
smooshed (143)

careening (150)
huz-huz (153)
unadulterated (160)
frilly (162)
whalloped (177)
reluctant (190)
ghastly (192)
noggin (193)
alpha and omega (201)
eyebrow-messages (202)
wing-ding (206)
redible (208)
nonchalantly (210)
vaporizing (219)
upsidey-down (224)
dinger (226)
defying (227)
percolating (234)
plonked (240)
extensively (240)
prejudgments (241)
noble (249)
bountiful (252)
whizzing (257)
hairpin (260)
metallic (262)
grotesquely (264)
gurgling (268)
magnify (277)

Pacific

★ **Alaska**
Toughboy and Sister
by Kirkpatrick Hill
(Puffin, 1990)

★ **Washington**
*Yang the Youngest
and His Terrible Ear*
by Lensey Namioka
(Yearling, 1994)

★ **Hawaii**
Under the Blood-Red Sun
by Graham Salisbury
(Yearling, 1994)

★ **Oregon**
The Barn
by Avi
(Avon, 1994)

★ **California**
The Ballad of Lucy Whipple
by Karen Cushman
(HarperCollins, 1996)

Other Recommended Regional Readings

★ **Alaska**

Julie of the Wolves by Jean Craighead George
(HarperTrophy, 1972)

★ **California**

Baseball in April and Other Stories by Gary
Soto (Harcourt, 1990)

Cat Running by Zilpha Keatley Snyder (Dell,
1994)

Downwind by Louise Moeri (Dell, 1984)

I Am Lavina Cumming by Susan Lowell
(Milkweed, 1993) (Arizona,California)

Riding Freedom by Pam Munoz Ryan
(Scholastic, 1998)

★ **Hawaii**

Jungle Dogs by Graham Salisbury (Bantam,
1998)

★ **Oregon**

The Ghost Stallion by Laura E. Williams
(Holt, 1999)

★ **Washington**

Ghost Canoe by Will Hobbs (Morrow, 1997)

Turtle People by Brenda Guiberson
(Atheneum, 1990)

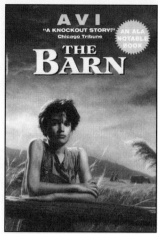

 **Recorded Books**

Summary

It's 1855 in Oregon Territory. Benjamin may be only nine years old and the youngest in his family, but he's also definitely the smartest. That's why he's away at school when his father is stricken with "a fit of palsy." Back home, Ben takes charge of caring for Father—cleaning him, painstakingly feeding him—while his older sister and brother work the fields on the claim. That's when Ben realizes that Father can communicate by blinking his eyes and that Father wants them to build a barn. Ben becomes convinced that he and Father have an agreement: They will build the barn and Father will get well.

Background

The young Avi Wortis was a poor writer during high school and still has papers full of red marks from his teachers. A tutor helped him nurture his dream of becoming a writer, and Avi is now known as an inventive, adventuresome author who has experimented with a number of different forms and has been recognized with several Newbery Honor awards.

This novel is a spare yet lyrical book, great for readers who need short books with much to reflect on. The short last scene of the novel takes place seventy years later. At that point, Ben

realizes the barn—as Father promised—is "something fine to come home to. Still standing. Still strong." Discuss with students why the author might have decided that scene was important to include. If you are able to visit a nursing home, students may gain some insight into what Ben's task of caring for his father is like.

 **Book Pairing**

Many books are available with details of the journey over the Oregon Trail. *If You Traveled West in a Covered Wagon* by Ellen Levine (Scholastic, 1986) is a nonfiction book that uses a question/answer format; *The West: An Illustrated History for Children* by Dayton Duncan (Little Brown, 1996) is another nonfiction book with a good description of the trail with pictures. *Bound for Oregon* by Jean Van Leeuwen (Dial, 1994) and *I'm Sorry, Almira Ann* by Jane Kurtz (Holt, 1999) are two fiction books that include many real details of daily life on the trail.

Find Out More

About the author "Learning About Avi" by eighth-grade teacher Megan Hall from Kay Vandergrift's <u>Learning About Authors/Illustrators Pages</u> at **http://www.scils.rutgers.edu/special/kay/avi.html** provides background about the author with some specific comments on *The Barn*.

The Oregon Trail *The Story of the Oregon Trail* (VHS), directed by Steven Boettcher (originally shown on PBS) is an excellent classroom resource. Ordering information can be found at The Oregon Trail at **http://www.isu.edu/~trinmich/Oregontrail.html**.

Hands-on Activities

Map it During the 1800s, more than 300,000 people, including Ben's family, headed west on the Oregon Trail. Help students locate maps that show different routes west that pioneer families like Ben's might have taken. Have them recreate a route map that shows one possible route Ben's family might have used to get to Oregon. (Note references to where the family started on page 10.)

Life on the trail After students have created their route map of Ben's family's journey, invite them to write a scene in which Ben is sitting with his father and talking about their trip to the West Coast and how they ended up in Oregon. Suggest that students use books from the Book Pairing or these Web sites to help them with their research:

The Oregon Trail at **http://www.isu.edu/~trinmich/Oregontrail.html**
American West at **http://www.americanwest.com/trails/pages/oretrail.htm**
Oregon Trail Project at **http://cnug.clackesd.k12.or.us/oretrail/ot.html**

Students' stories can be hung beside the maps to create a display of both geographic and historical-fiction perspectives of life on the trail.

Stars and stripes in history Ben refers to the fact that he and his family live in Oregon Territory (page 6). Challenge students to find out when Oregon became a state. Then have groups draw a representation of the U.S. flag both before and after Oregon's statehood. Refer students to The Flags of the United States of America at **http://www.usflag.org/toc.flags.html**, which shows the evolution of the flag.

Cornhusk dolls—a link to the past On page 15, Ben says that Father made him think of "an old corn husk doll without stuffing." To familiarize students with this old-time reference, show students how to make cornhusk dolls. Two resources that provide history and directions for creating these crafts are *Cornhusk, Silk, and Wishbones: A Book of Dolls from Around the World* by Michelle Markel (Clarion, 2000) and *How to Make Corn Husk Dolls* by Ruth Wendorff (Arco, 1973). Arrange for students to take their dolls to a nursing home in your community to give to the residents there. Perhaps some people in the nursing home will remember making cornhusk dolls and be willing to provide students with some historical perspective on how this doll was a product of their early lives. After you get back to the classroom, discuss what you discovered.

Charting the weather Ben talks about clouds (page 35), rain (page 49), wind and fog (page 55), and flood (page 72) in his part of the country. Ask students to study the weather map in the local newspaper and explain the purpose and meanings of the legends and what kinds of information can be found on such maps. (You can also direct them to the Weather Channel or to **http://excite.com** or to **http://yahoo.com** on the Internet.) Design a three-week chart in which students compare such things as the high and low temperatures, cloudiness, and rainfall in your community and the Northwest. Students can find information about Oregon weather patterns under "Oregon" in the *World Book Encyclopedia*.

How to build a barn Ben describes the way he uses the geometry he learned in school to build the barn (pages 67–71) and hoist the beam (page 97). Check students' attention to details and their ability to display procedural knowledge with this diagramming activity. Have students reread these sections and then draw a diagram or build a model that will illustrate what he figures out.

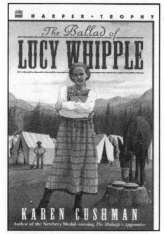

 Recorded Books

The Ballad of Lucy Whipple

Karen Cushman

HarperCollins, 1996

Summary

California Morning Whipple could not be more miserable in gold-rush California, the land of her parents' dreams (which accounts for her name). She misses her pa, buried in the soil of faraway Massachusetts, and everything about home. Though her no-nonsense mother will not tolerate complaints or her daughter's being "notional," the narrator takes steps to remedy things: She renames herself Lucy and sets out to earn enough money to get back home. Can she bake enough pies, loan out enough books, or think of enough schemes to return to Massachusetts?

Background

Karen Cushman won a Newbery Honor for her first novel, *Catherine, Called Birdy* (Trophy Newbery, 1995) and a Newbery Award for her second, *The Midwife's Apprentice* (Trophy Newbery, 1996). This is her third novel. *The Ballad of Lucy Whipple* combines Cushman's strong interest in creating characters, writing fiction, and exploring key historical events—in this case, the gold rush.

In the early days of the gold rush, one person wrote home that his young girls could make $5 to $25 every day by washing gold in pans. After almost 100,000 people rushed to California in 1849, riverbanks were crowded with prospectors and surface gold was soon gone. After that, men

had to dig deeper and deeper. Many who made their fortunes did so by becoming entrepreneurs serving the people who were hunting for gold. For instance, Levi Strauss, a German immigrant, moved to San Francisco with some cotton material he planned to use for tents—and ended up making sturdy pants for miners. In 1851, one of the 20,000 Chinese people in California opened the first San Francisco hand laundry.

  Book Pairing

Use the nonfiction resource *The West: An Illustrated History for Children* by Dayton Duncan (Little, Brown, 1996) to highlight stories of historic figures and key events from the gold rush era.

Find Out More

About the author HarperChildrens.com at **http://www.harperchildrens.com/school house/TeachersGuides/cushmanindex.htm** features an interview with Karen Cushman along with a teaching guide for *The Ballad of Lucy Whipple*.

The gold rush Find facts and activities at Center X at **http://www.centerx.gseis.ucla.edu/out reach/projects/chssp/bpsources/Gold_rush/ goldrush1.html**.

Hands-on Activities

Graphic organizer: All That Glitters is Not Gold: A Massachusetts/California Comparison (page 103) Start a class discussion about the way Lucy is always thinking back to how things were and what she has lost. Have students use evidence from the book to compare and contrast Lucy's new life with the one she left behind when her family moved. Students can fill in the comparison matrix with details about Lucy's experiences with food, education, housing, and education and books in these two disparate places.

Map it Using a U.S. map as a model and Cushman's descriptions to guide them, students can create a route map that shows Lucy Whipple's journey from Massachusetts to California and her planned journey back to Massachusetts. Have students use different colors to distinguish her actual trip to California and her planned trip back. They can enhance the map with symbols that show her method of transportation for each leg of the journey. Show students how to include a legend for the map to define the symbols and colors they use.

Route back home When Lucy's mother gets fed up and takes a day off, leaving Lucy in charge, Lucy goes off to find wood and gets lost. Have students make a map to help Lucy find her way back home, starting at Lucky Diggins and including all her day's wanderings (page 68).

Dear Lucy The rest of Lucy's family finally leaves California to move to the Sandwich Islands. Encourage students to look up the Sandwich Islands in the *World Book Encyclopedia*, locate them the islands on a map, and investigate them further. Then have them use their research to write a letter from Lucy's younger sister Sierra to Lucy describing Sierra's new life after she leaves California.

The Whipple story Lucy says, "Did you ever stop to think that someday we will be history, part of the great Gold Search or some such?" (page 81). Seek out books in your library media center that describe the gold rush (see Book Pairing selection). Have students select a book and write a paragraph describing the experience of the Whipple family of Lucky Diggins that could be added to the book. Where would it fit in (which chapter and page)?

Cross-country in a flash? Nineteenth-century transportation time line During the gold rush, boys and young men on horseback would dash into the camps carrying the mail. Students will enjoy learning about how the letters, newspapers, books, and magazines they received and the mail they sent was transported from the East to California. In 1860, William Russell came up with an idea to deliver mail in 10 days, much faster than the usual 25. Most of the boys who answered the ad for "young, skinny, wiry fellows, not over 18" had grown up on the frontier and were good horsemen. Each was given a bright red shirt and blue pants, a horn to signal the relay station, two guns, and a Bible. The Pony Express lasted only about 18 months and lost about $200,000 as a business, but it is still remembered. Make a time line showing the heyday periods of covered wagons, the Pony Express, stagecoaches, and train travel between the East/Midwest and California.

American folk songs and poetry Lucy mentions many songs, including "Sweet Betsy from Pike," "Turkey in the Straw," "Amazing Grace," "Woodman Spare That Tree," "Home Sweet Home," "Oh Suzanna," and "Maryland, My Maryland." You can find lyrics for many of them in your library media center. Tracey West's *Teaching American History With Favorite Folk Songs* (Scholastic, 2001) includes an audio recording of songs from the time of Westward Expansion with lyrics and teaching activities. Encourage students to write words for their own songs about what they've learned from their reading and research, using familiar tunes as a structure.

All That Glitters is Not Gold:
A Massachusetts/California Comparison

The Ballad of Lucy Whipple

Lucy is always thinking back to how things were and what she has lost. Review the *The Ballad of Lucy Whipple* to compare and contrast Lucy's new life with the one she left behind when her family moved. Then fill in the chart below to show how Lucy's memories of food, housing, and education and books from Massachusetts compare with her daily life in California.

	Massachusetts	California
Food		
Housing		
Education/Books		

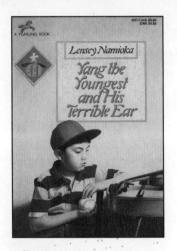

Yang the Youngest and His Terrible Ear

Lensey Namioka

Yearling, 1992

Summary

Eldest Brother plays the violin beautifully. Yang the Second Eldest can create a rainbow of notes with the viola. Yang the Third Eldest washes her listeners in deep, mellow cello notes. But Yang the Youngest, Yingtao, draws his bow across the violin strings and produces a "screech." Yingtao picks up American ways quickly, including how to play baseball, but nothing can turn him into the accomplished musician his father expects him to be, while nothing can turn his best friend, Matthew, into the baseball player *his* father wants him to be.

Background

Lensey Namioka grew up reading adventure stories in her mother's Chinese pulp novels. Namioka "and her sisters made up their own tales of valiant sword-fighting outlaws to amuse one another after the family's move to the United States during World War II." Namioka taught college math before turning to writing and credits her style of writing to her mathematics background. Many of her books have a theme of tolerance, but the author also believes that "the more important an author's message, the more fun her book should be." You can add to that feeling of fun by exploring the five senses before or during the reading of *Yang the Youngest and His Terrible Ear*. For instance, listen to a string quartet, taste a persimmon, look at an inkstone or Chinese painting, try eating with chopsticks.

 Book Pairing

Many picture books take a look at pieces of the immigrant experience. *How My Parents Learned to Eat* by Ina R. Friedman (Houghton Mifflin, 1984) shows subtle similarities and differences in cultural experiences. *Faraway Home* by Jane Kurtz (Harcourt, 2000) shows what it's like when a child thinks of the U.S. as home while her parents still consider home to be another country. *Grandfather's Journey* by Allen Say (Houghton Mifflin, 1993) explores that reality of many immigrant lives—a person who ends up homesick no matter where he chooses to live. *Nim and the War Effort* by Milly Lee (Farrar, Straus & Giroux, 1997) shows a child adapting to life in the U.S. but upsetting her traditional grandfather's sense of propriety.

Find Out More

About the author YRCA Sample Book Ideas at **http://www.acs.ucalgary.ca/~dkbrown/ yrca_namioka.html** offers author background, book links, a recipe for fortune cookies, and other activities related to this book.

China The Lensey Namioka page from McGraw-Hill at **http://www.mhschool.com/student/ reading/mhreading/6/6-1-3.html** provides links to the art of China and Chinese calligraphy, daily life in Ancient China, and more.

Seattle Materials that can enhance students' understanding of the book's setting include a

visitor's guide to Seattle available through Seattle-King County Center and Visitor's Bureau, 520 Pike St, Suite 1300, Seattle, WA 98101, 206-461-5840, and on the Internet at **http://www.seattleinsider.com/partners/seeseattle/**.

Baseball If students are relatively unfamiliar with baseball, guide them to resources that tell the story of baseball from different American perspectives, such as *Home Run: The Story of Babe Ruth* by Robert Burleigh (Harcourt, 1998) and *Baseball Saved Us* by Ken Mochizuki (Lee & Low, 1993).

Korean-American links Yingtao's teacher seats him next to a Korean girl, but they have nothing in common (page 20). To find out more about Korean Americans, visit the Web site of children's author Haemi Balgassi at **http://www.Haemi Balgassi. com)**, a Korean-American children's author. Her page has links to other pages about Korea and Korean Americans.

Invite a speaker Invite a speaker to your class who has moved to the United States from another country and would be comfortable discussing that experience. Afterward, lead a discussion about the similarities and differences between the speaker's and the Yang family's experiences.

Hands-on Activities

Graphic organizer: Survival Skills: Living in Seattle (page 106) Discuss with students the kinds of knowledge and skills Yingtao possessed that helped him survive in many new situations in Seattle. Ask them to consider what knowledge and skills he didn't have that would have helped him to survive more easily. Then have students fill out the organizer with specific skills Yingtao possessed or could have used in baseball, at school, in his home life, with the string quartet, and at his friend Matt's house. Remind students to use passages from the book for support.

Map it Break out the atlases and ask students to locate Shanghai in China and Seattle in the United States. How far did the Yang family have to fly? For an instant measurement, send students to Indo.com at **http://www. indo.com/distance/**. If you'd like students to calculate the distance on their own, have them stretch string across the map from Seattle to Shanghai and use a map scale and ruler to find the distance.

Idiom game Yingtao says, "Talking to Americans is like walking along a country footpath in China. You think the path is nice and firm, but your foot suddenly slips on a muddy stretch and you land with a big splash in a wet rice paddy" (page 60). With students, generate a list of the American idioms that Yang's family thinks are confusing. Have students each choose one idiom to illustrate, showing its literal meaning. Then they can trade cards and try to guess the idioms.

Shanghai-Seattle scrapbook Have students skim the book for setting details and then create a scrapbook that the Yang family might have kept of sights around Shanghai and then sights of Seattle after the move. Encourage students to visit the Shanghai Vista site at **http://www.chinavista.com/shanghai/links. html** and the Visiting Seattle site at **http://www.cityofseattle.net/html/visitor/**.

Class-y humor In a starred review of *Yang the Youngest and His Terrible Ear, Publishers Weekly* praised Lensey Namioka's "comedic timing." Find examples of funny spots in the book and show students how Namioka creates that "comedic timing." To support the discussion, if possible, invite a comedian to come to class to talk about timing—or play a videotape of someone telling jokes well. Then let students practice telling jokes. Finally, have them use Namioka's writing techniques to create the jokes on paper, capturing such things as the pause before the punch line.

Survival Skills: Living in Seattle

Yang the Youngest and His Terrible Ear

What knowledge and skills did Yingtao have that helped him adjust to baseball, school, string quartet, his home life, and the customs he encounters at his friend Matt's home? What knowledge and skills didn't he have that would have helped him to survive more easily? Fill in the chart with details for each category.

	Skills Yingtao Used to Survive in Seattle	Skills Yingtao Didn't Have That Would Have Helped Him
Baseball		
School		
Home		
Music (string quartet)		
Matt's house		

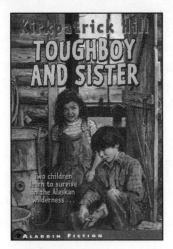

Toughboy and Sister

Kirkpatrick Hill

Puffin, 1990

Summary

Toughboy, who is nearly eleven, and his younger sister Annie Laurie, just called Sister, manage to stay with their father after their mother dies giving birth, despite the plans of the women in their Athabaskan village in Alaska. When summer comes again, the children head to Fish Camp with their father, but before their summer life gets underway, their father vanishes. Toughboy and Sister are forced to try to survive on their own, without a boat, with limited food and resources, with only their wits and each other to keep them alive.

Background

Kirkpatrick Hill knows the setting of this book well. She was raised in Fairbanks, Alaska. Even though she received her college degrees in English and Education in New York, she has taught elementary school for more than thirty years in multigrade classrooms or one-room schools in the Alaskan wilderness. She currently lives in Fairbanks, Alaska.

Book Pairing

If you'd like to learn more about native Alaskan culture and the importance of fishing, read *Salmon Summer* by Bruce McMillan (Houghton Mifflin, 1998) about an Aleut boy, and *Anna's Athabaskan Summer* by Arnold A. Griese (Boyds Mills Press, 1995) about an Athabaskan girl, both at fish camp.

Find Out More

Athabaskan culture Check out the following Internet resources:

★ A social studies unit "Athabascans of Interior Alaska" is available at the <u>Alaska Native Knowledge Network (ANKN)</u> site at **http://www.ankn.uaf.edu/Athabascan/ index.html**. Other sources of cultural information at the same site are on the "Alaska Native Cultural Resources: Athabascan" page at **http://www.ankn.uaf.edu/athabascan.html**.

★ Visit an Athabaskan village school in Koyukuk, Alaska, at **http://www.vernetti.koyukuk.k12. ak.us/vernettihome.htm**. On the wheel-shaped menu, click on Subsistence Living and follow links to Fishing or Hunting.

★ If you visit the <u>Fiddlechicks</u> site, you'll find a page devoted to Athabascan folk music at **http://www.fiddlechicks.com/athabascan. htm**. Here you can click on various links that will motivate students to learn more about Athabascan musicians and hear their music.

Hands-on Activities

Graphic organizer: Fish Camp Survival Skills (page 109) Prepare students to fill in this web on page 109 by leading them in a discussion about how elders can be an important resource in all cultures. Help students understand that elders teach the young what they need to know about the culture and its way of life. Students then should consider what knowledge and skills Toughboy and Sister's elders (including their parents) have passed on to them that help them to survive at Fish Camp—and what knowledge and skills they hadn't learned that would have made it easier for them to survive.

Map it With setting clues from the book and a map that details interior Alaska, students can locate the area of Alaska where Toughboy and Sister live, or they can create their own map of it. Point out that as students read the novel closely, they will find many names of places that will help to guide their map work, including Yukon River, Tanana, Galena, Kodiak, and Koyukuk.

Bulletin board: fish camp setting Have students review sections of the book that describe the fish camp. Work with the class to create a general map of the camp on the bulletin board. Let students work in pairs or groups to illustrate details about camp life, such as the cabin, cache, fish-cutting raft, wood lot, and cranberry patch, to add visual interest around the map. At each spot where a major event happens, have students place an arrow and attach a description of the event that takes place there.

Presenting procedural knowledge: how to cut and dry fish Alaska-style Download "Village Science" by Alan Dick, sponsored by the Alaska Native Knowledge Network, at **http://www.ankn.uaf.edu/vscover.html**. Chapter 1, "Cutting and Drying Fish," provides students with great background on the process that the Silas family used at fish camp.

Alaska terms vocabulary cards Many different languages are spoken by the native peoples of Alaska. (For a map of Alaska with the many languages marked, go to the ANKN Alaska Native Languages site at **http://www.ankn.uaf.edu/anl.html**.) Provide students with vocabulary support as they encounter the native words Kirkpatrick Hill uses in *Toughboy and Sister*. Have students search out the italicized words in the book and write each word on an index card with a definition they've developed using the context clues that Hill gives in her book. Extend the activity by having students alphabetize the cards, illustrate them, and keep them in a box or staple them together to make a dictionary of these words.

Black bear board game Begin planning your game by assigning students to research the species of black bear that live in Alaska. The "Alaska Bear Pictures" page has pictures and useful information about bear behavior at **http://alaska-bear-pictures.com/index.html**, or you can visit Alaskan.com, which has a page of tips about staying safe from black bears at **http://www.alaskan.com/docs/bearsnyou.html**. Students should make a list of five facts that they know about Alaskan black bears from the novel and then add five more facts that they learn through their research. Using other board game structures as models, challenge student groups to create a board game in which Toughboy and Sister try to outsmart the black bear near fish camp. They can use the facts they've collected to create the "chance" or "fate" cards that set back or advance players and to make the squares on the game board.

Letter to Old Natasha Extend the graphic organizer activity by inviting students to write to Old Natasha in the voices of Toughboy and Sister. Students should have each character describe, from his or her point of view, what he or she is grateful to know and be able to do, and what he or she longed to have known or been able to do.

Fish Camp Survival Skills
Toughboy and Sister

What knowledge and skills did Toughboy and Sister use to survive at Fish Camp? What knowledge and skills didn't they have that would have helped them to survive more easily? Fill in this web with examples of their knowledge and skills in these areas: finding food, water, and shelter and protecting themselves from nature.

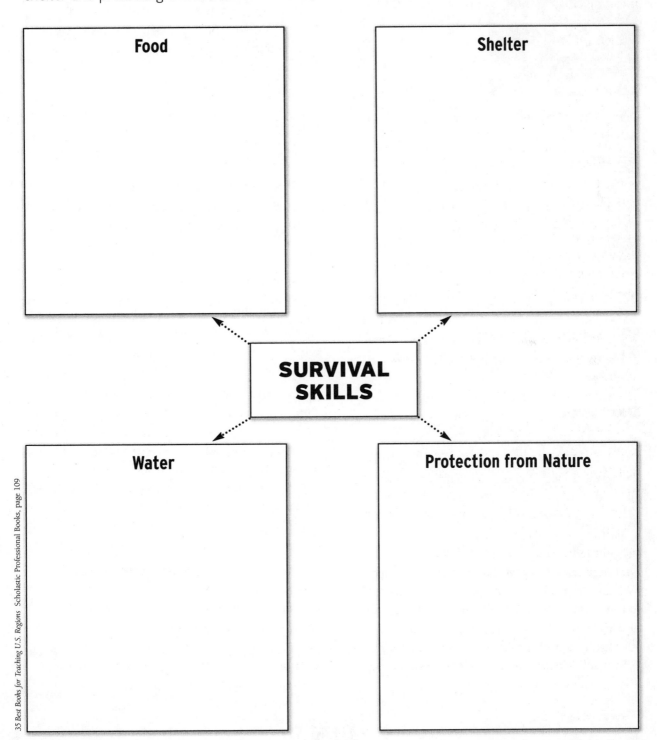

Food

Shelter

SURVIVAL SKILLS

Water

Protection from Nature

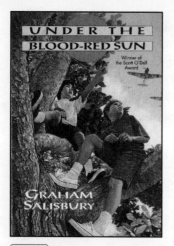

 Recorded Books

Under the Blood-Red Sun
Graham Salisbury
Yearling, 1994

Summary

Hawaiian-born Tomi and his sister Kimi are living on the island of Oahu, Hawaii, with their Japanese immigrant parents and grandfather, when Pearl Harbor is attacked on December 7, 1941. Anti-Japanese sentiment explodes. Tomi's father is arrested, leaving 13-year-old Tomi in charge of the family, when all he really wants to do is to play baseball and enjoy his friends. It is a difficult time to be Japanese; Tomi must struggle to preserve his cultural heritage while defining for himself what it means to be an American.

Background

After the Japanese bombed Pearl Harbor on December 7, 1941, President Franklin Delano Roosevelt issued Executive Order 9066, which allowed the evacuation and mass imprisonment of 120,000 people of Japanese-American descent in hastily constructed internment camps surrounded by barbed wire and guarded by armed guards. They were forced to leave their jobs and their homes and were interned for up to four years. Most of these people were citizens of the United States or permanent resident aliens; many of them were children. In this story, Tomi's father is one of the interned.

 Book Pairing

Not only adults, like Tomi's father, were confined in Japanese-American internment camps—children were, too. Have students read *The Children of Topaz: The Story of a Japanese-American Internment Camp Based on a Classroom Diary* by Michael O. Tunnell (Holiday House, 1996) to learn about children who were interned during the period in which Tomi's story takes place.

Find Out More

About the author Graham Salisbury grew up on the islands of Oahu and Hawaii. You can learn more about him and his books at his personal Web site at **http://www.grahamsalisbury.com/**.

Literature guide Random House.com offers "Images of War: A Special Issue Teacher's Guide from Random House Teacher's Guides" at **http://www.randomhouse.com/teachers/guides/imagesofwar.html**, which includes a prereading activity, multiple classroom connections, and discussion question.

Internment camps and children The PBS site at **http://www.children-of-the-camps.org/** is devoted to the documentary film *Children of the Camps*, which portrays the internment of six Japanese-American children by the U.S. government during World War II.

Pearl Harbor Find "Remembering Pearl Harbor: The USS Arizona Memorial," at the National Register of Historic Places Teaching with Historic

Places site at **http://www.cr.nps.gov/nr/twhp/ wwwlps/lessons/18arizona/18arizona.htm**. This extensive lesson will offer students background information that they are not likely to have about Pearl Harbor, including the logistics of the Japanese attack and the Arizona's destruction. You'll also find maps, readings, charts, photos, and supplementary activities.

Social studies connection You can find a social studies mini-unit focused on *Under the Blood-Red Sun* developed by Lynette B. Reeder, located at the TeacherLINK on-line teacher resource center maintained by Utah State University at **http://teacherlink.ed.usu.edu/TLresources/ longterm/LessonPlans/socst/LBREEDER/ summaryw.html**.

Hands-on Activities

Map it Have students draw a map of the island of Oahu, Hawaii. Tell students to show important sites mentioned in the book, such as Honolulu Harbor, which is near Tomi's house, and Pearl Harbor. If students use the Internet for their research, direct them to the Best of Hawaii site at **http://www.bestofhawaii. com/map_oahu.htm** for a detailed map.

Flags around the world Flags play an important role in this novel and in many people's lives. Create a flag display with a large world map and student-drawn flags. Have students choose a flag that they have a special connection with or that they simply like, make a small replica of the flag from craft paper, and then post it on a map of the world, marking the country it belongs to. You can print out small flags to color at the Colouring Book of Flags site at **http://www.crwflags.com/fotw/ flags/cbk.html**.

Amazing pigeons Tomi and his grandfather raise pigeons. Throughout history, the military has used pigeons to help them with their work, especially in World War I and World War II. Challenge students to find out why. Your library media center may have several books about pigeons that students will enjoy, including a fictional picture book, *Language of the Doves* by Rosemary Wells (Dial, 1996). Students also can find information on pigeons at "Pigeon Pages" on the Urban Wildlife Society site at **http:// www.goodnet.com/~animals/pigeons/**. (While they are there, encourage students to take the "Gee Whiz Animal Quiz.")

Pigeon poetry Introduce students to haiku, a form of Japanese poetry consisting of three lines with a 5-7-5 syllable pattern. You'll find great poems to read aloud in *Cricket Never Does: A Collection of Haiku and Tanka* by Myra Cohn Livingston (McElderry, 1997). After students have researched pigeons and gathered many facts about them, they can write their own pigeon haiku, which you can collect to create a class book.

Mr. Nakaji's letters home After students have done some reading about the internment camps, challenge them to imagine that they are Mr. Nakaji writing a letter home to his wife, father, and children. What can he tell the family about his arrest and his life in the camp? Make sure students include as much authentic detail as possible.

Hot off the press Engage students in an examination of bias by having them write two newspaper articles, each from a different perspective. In the first article, to be published in a newspaper run by the Japanese community, they should report the imprisonment of Tomi's father and other Japanese men. In the second article, to be published in a non-Japanese Hawaiian newspaper, they should report the same incident. Share some of the contrasting articles and discuss how the cultural background and experiences of the writer can lead to such different perspectives.

Japanese terms dictionary Throughout _Under the Blood-Red Sun,_ Graham Salisbury sprinkles Japanese words such as _haole_, _katana_, and _butsudan_. Have students record these terms as they encounter them and create a dictionary of these Japanese words. Remind students to draw their definitions from the context of the passage in which they find the word.